My Childhood in Pieces

My Childhood in Pieces

A STAND-UP COMEDY, A SKOKIE ELEGY

Edward Hirsch

ALFRED A. KNOPF

NEW YORK

2025

A BORZOI BOOK
FIRST HARDCOVER EDITION
PUBLISHED BY ALFRED A. KNOPF 2025

Published by Alfred A. Knopf, a division of Penguin Random House
LLC, 1745 Broadway, New York NY 10019.

Knopf, Borzoi Books, and the colophon are registered trademarks
of Penguin Random House LLC.

All photographs in text are courtesy of the author.

LIBRARY OF CONGRESS CATALOGING-IN-PUBLICATION DATA
Names: Hirsch, Edward, author.
Title: My childhood in pieces : a stand-up comedy, a Skokie elegy /
Edward Hirsch.
Description: First edition. | New York : Alfred A. Knopf, [2025] |
Identifiers: LCCN 2024030424 (print) | LCCN 2024030425 (ebook)
| ISBN 9780593802823 (hardcover) | ISBN 9781524712686 (trade
paperback) | ISBN 9780593802830 (ebook)
Subjects: LCSH: Hirsch, Edward—Childhood and youth. | Hirsch,
Edward—Family. | Poets, American—20th century—Biography. |
Jews—Illinois—Skokie—Biography. | Skokie (Ill.) —Biography.
Classification: LCC PS3558.I64 Z46 2025 (print) | LCC PS3558.I64
(ebook) | DDC 811/.54 [B] —dc23/eng/20241016
LC record available at https://lccn.loc.gov/2024030424
LC ebook record available at https://lccn.loc.gov/2024030425

penguinrandomhouse.com | aaknopf.com

Printed in the United States of America
2 4 6 8 9 7 5 3 1

The authorized representative in the EU for product safety
and compliance is Penguin Random House Ireland, Morrison
Chambers, 32 Nassau Street, Dublin D02 YH68, Ireland,
https://eu-contact.penguin.ie.

for Arlene Hirsch, the two of us

and Nancy Hirsch, and then the three of us

My Childhood in Pieces

PROLOGUE

My grandparents taught me to write my sins on paper and cast them into the water on the first day of the New Year. They didn't expect an entire book.

1

ALL SALES ARE FINAL

"God is like my old boss on Maxwell Street," my grandfather said. "You may get home and discover that your new shirt doesn't have a back, but you're still not going to get a refund."

TWO DAUGHTERS

My grandparents Oscar and Anna Ginsburg had two daughters, Irma and Bernice. Irma was considered the smart one, Bernice the pretty one. From a mental-health perspective, it was easier to be the pretty one.

A DAUGHTER, A SON

My grandparents Ellis and Elsie Rubenstein had two children, Elaine and Harold. Elaine was considered the princess, Harold the hustler. From a mental-health perspective, it was easier to be the princess.

IT'S ALL RELATIVE

My grandparents Oscar and Anna helped raise me. My grandmother Elsie died before I was born. My grandfather Ellis keeled over before I was a year old.

HOW MY MOTHER LEARNED TO SWIM

A choppy day on Lake Michigan in the summer of 1935. My grandmother threw her off the pier and told her to keep her head above the waves.

JUNIOR HIGH ROMANCE

Harold and Irma started going together in seventh grade. Everyone in school called him Ruby. She did too. They danced at his bar mitzvah. That was fateful. They went to Charles R. Darwin Public School. It was elementary. They didn't know much about the English naturalist. They did know it was survival of the fittest.

HIGH SCHOOL ROMANCE

Irma and Ruby moved up to Theodore Roosevelt High School. They were Rough Riders. She was quick in school. He was not. She pulled him through. He was quick in other things. He taught her them.

PETTING

Look at them making out on the kitchen floor. They called it *petting*. Irma's little sister Bea stepped over them for a snack. Her mother said, "What are you, farm animals?"

SIDE BY SIDE

Ruby and Irma worked side by side in Baker's Shoes. She sold purses and gloves. She knew women's hands. She worked the cash register. She was the honest one. Ruby sold discount shoes and hustled shoe polish. He knew women's feet. He wasn't allowed near the cash register. He was not the honest one. The honest one and the not-so-honest one had fun together. They could cut up. One thing leads to another. That other thing leads to marriage.

TAGALONG

Irma kept a careful eye on Bea. She didn't like dragging her along, but she didn't like leaving her behind either. She especially disliked it when her younger sister skipped ahead. "There goes Bea with the bony knee."

GIRL IN A SHOE STORE

Bea was eleven when she took over Irma's post in the shoe store. She was tall and looked like a teenager. It was a cushy job. She refused to give it back after the school year.

When she turned twelve, Bea confessed to the manager that she was not sixteen. She was tearful. Mr. Spivak said, "Do you know how much trouble I could get in for hiring a minor? You're not getting a raise."

THE RULE BURNED

Irma and Ruby moved over to Maling Shoes. The situation was the same. The boys could sell anything. The girls could not sell women's shoes.

The rule burned the two sisters. The younger sister accepted it, the older one seethed.

TWO SIDES OF THE BOULEVARD

Palmer Square is a pocket of Logan Square inside northwest Chicago inside Cook County inside northeastern Illinois. Harold and Irma were cooked there in the 1930s and '40s.

Palmer Square was once called Palmer Place. Ruby's family was well placed to one side of it. Irma's family was not well placed on the other. A wide boulevard separated them.

Irma could spy Ruby's three-flat from her window. She almost never went there.

Ruby's parents didn't think much of Irma. Aunt Becky and Auntie Aya ran the household. They considered her an intruder.

Ruby didn't need to look for Irma's second-floor apartment. He was there all the time.

Irma's parents had a divided opinion about her boyfriend. And everything else.

My grandmother was a card shark. She liked the way Ruby played his hand. He was grounded and sporty. She thought he was a perfect match.

My grandfather was a daydreamer. He thought Ruby had bad blood because his father kept a mistress. He would have preferred someone up there in the clouds with him.

ISLAND OF PARADISE

After high school, Ruby got drafted into the army and sent to Camp Asan, which had been converted into a Civil Service camp, on the island of Guam. Since he was the only person in his unit who did not drink, he was put in charge of liquor for the PX. This made him the most powerful private in paradise.

After nine months, Private Rubenstein received a dependency discharge to take care of his ailing father, and paradise was lost.

WHAT'S THE DEAL?

Irma attended Roosevelt College. It was a brand-new school named after FDR, and she wanted a New Deal. But she dropped out after one year when her father had a heart attack. It was the same Old Deal. She needed to earn money to support her family.

THE EDGEWATER BEACH HOTEL

Irma and Ruby walked on Edgewater's private beach a few weeks before their wedding. It was a bracing day in early November. The lavish pink hotel looked as if it had been transported from Spain. It was like getting married in the Mediterranean. I see why their heads were turned, but why didn't they get cold feet?

BEFORE THANKSGIVING

Irma and Ruby got married on Thanksgiving Eve, 1948. She had turned twenty-one. He was a few weeks away. Since he was under-age, Ruby needed his father to sign for him. His father was a hard drinker, and it was the heaviest drinking night of the year. He signed.

ON THE MATRIMONIAL BATTLEFRONT

There was no honeymoon for Harold, whose name means "Army Ruler," and Irma, whose name means "God's Warrior Princess."

HARMONY OF THE FACE

No one wanted Irma to get a nosejob. Her parents were against it, her sister was against it, her friends were against it, and her husband was against it.

Her three children would have been against it, too, but we weren't born yet.

Irma would not be dissuaded. She never regretted it.

She did regret waking up during the procedure. She heard them crack her nose. Then they put her back to sleep.

When she woke up, she had a new face.

APRIL FOOLS' DAY

No joke, Irma and Ruby thought they were ready for a child. The joke was on them. It was also on me. I had a joke played on me before I was born. Can you have a practical joke played on you before you are conceived?

THE GAMBLER

The guys were playing cards on the night my mother's water broke. She needed to get to the hospital immediately. It was snowing outside. "I'll just call you a cab and finish the game," my father said, "I've got a good hand."

ONE WINTER NIGHT IN BRONZEVILLE

I was born at 2 a.m. at Michael Reese Hospital on the Near South Side of Chicago. It was a Friday in the Year of the Tiger. My mother said she was having a nightmare.

AVENUE OF THE FATHER

Ruby was having a nightmare too. The hospital was located on Ellis Avenue. He didn't like his father, Ellis. But he couldn't escape him either.

ELSIE / EDWARD

Ruby's mother, Elsie, never recovered from giving birth to him. She was bedridden with a heart murmur. Everyone blamed him. He felt guilty. He named me after her.

MAKING A MARK

My parents gave me the middle name *Mark* because it sounded classy. They didn't know it derives from the Latin name *Mars*, god of war. But they were embattled.

IN THE NURSERY

"I started to sob when the nurse pointed you out in the nursery," Auntie Bea told me. "I had never seen such a strange-looking infant. You were all eyes and nose, and your face trailed behind. Your hair was spiky. You were emaciated. You looked like you were born in an alley."

FAMILY RESEMBLANCE

All my life people have said that I look like Bea.

BABY BOOM

"It was loud," my mom told me. "You've always been a crier. With you, it was baby boom, bang, and blast."

THE COMEDIAN

"I gave birth to you on January 20th," my mom explained, "just so you could have the same birthday as George Burns." I didn't know who that was. "He's Gracie Allen's sidekick," she said. "Don't be funny."

TWO JEWISH MOTHERS

According to Genesis, Sarah laughed when she found out she was giving birth to a son. At least my mom waited until afterwards.

AND GOD SPOKE

It was as if God spoke to Irma in a dream. He said, "You have a newborn son. He should become a doctor."

"But what if he is not good in science?" Irma asked.

And God spoke again: "He should become a tax attorney."

CONFUSION IN THE CRIB

My mom said I was listening closely when she vowed that I would never play football because it's too dangerous. She also told me that I should never say never.

MAKING THE CUT

I once met a man who made me scream. He carried a little black box of instruments and mumbled mumbo jumbo over my body. It was the mohel who circumcised me.

SECOND HAND

My sister Arlene was born on a Sunday night in March 1951. My father was playing cards and wanted to finish the hand. My mom went to Michael Reese on her own. It was a long draw. He rushed to the hospital. He got there just in time. It was the only time.

TWO ANNAS

Arlene was named after Ruby's grandmother Anna. We didn't know anything about her. But our mom's mom was named Anna too and we loved her. We just transferred what we knew about one Anna to what we didn't know about the other.

BLAME GAME

My mom said she named my sister for her nickname, which she spelled Lenie. Everyone leaned into calling her *Leanie*. She was a cute little butterball. It wasn't her fault she looked like Ruby's family.

MILK

My mother wouldn't be cowed into nursing. She believed that bodily functions were unseemly. Breastfeeding was unsanitary. What could be healthier than formula? Milk was bottled for us.

POETIC IDEA OF EARLY CHILDHOOD

Source I cannot remember, exile I cannot forget.

WHAT LASTS

All their lives they carried the heat of first love plus the rage of early betrayal.

————

IRVING PARK

Our neighborhood on the Northwest Side was originally called Irvington. The name was a tribute to the author Washington Irving. But there was another Illinois town with the same name. Overnight, the place was changed to Irving Park. The whole neighborhood went to bed. It woke up and forgot about literature.

THE RIP VAN WINKLE EFFECT

Lenie and I grew up to be readers. As a lifelong insomniac, I could not relate to Irving's story of Rip Van Winkle, who falls asleep and wakes up twenty years later in a changed world. But he was my sister's personal hero. She would have gladly gone to bed and gotten up two decades later in a college dorm.

ZAYDE ELLIS

My parents lived with Ruby's father when they were first married. It was his apartment on West Byron Street. He did what he wanted. He was a smelter who smoked cigars and drank whiskey straight. Ruby had trouble deciding who was cruder, his dad or his dad's girlfriend.

A METALLURGIST

"You make money too fast," Ruby's father said. "You need to slow down." He wanted Harold to become a metallurgist. But Harold had no interest in studying materials science. He did not want to slow down and research metal. He wanted to go fast and peddle it.

DYING AT HOME

There was commotion in the apartment. Everyone knew Ruby's father was terminally ill; no one expected him to die.

Both of Ruby's parents passed away in their own beds. He was orphaned at home.

ELLIS SMELTING

My father inherited his father's white-metal smelting business. It was the Korean War. He could smell the money. Aluminum was the new metal in town. He was at the red-hot center. There were exciting exotic alloys. He knew how to get material. He could make a penny a pound on a deal. He was moving tons. He got rich quick.

LEADEN

Ruby started running with an older crowd. He had loose cash and flashy taste. He wore a gold necklace, a blue sapphire pinky ring. He had a wife and two children. We were leaden. He scrapped us.

NOUVEAU RICHE

My mother wanted no part of Ruby's new friends. She thought they were nouveau riche narcissists and status seekers. He didn't disagree. He just didn't see the problem.

SOME BILLS

Ruby didn't like waiting in line at a crowded restaurant. He tipped the maître d' two or three sawbucks—whatever did the trick—and his group was seated right away.

The upstarts were boisterous. Everyone ordered everything. Ruby picked up the tab for the table.

My mom complained that the bill cost more than the groceries. Ruby didn't care. What's the fun in popping for cereal?

My mom needed money for the kids. Ruby shrugged and peeled off some bills. That was a different kind of charge.

SIDENOTE

Ruby disapproved of female maître d's at the front of the house. They were harder to bribe.

A COUPLE OF PROVERBS

A watched kettle never boils. An unwatched kettle blows its top.

THE APOLOGY

Ruby disappeared for a week at a time. No one knew where he was. My mom guessed he was playing cards somewhere or other. If he won, he came home with a frilly pink dress for Lenie. He left the tag on to flaunt the price. This was his idea of an apology.

ON THE DRESSER

Ruby emptied his pockets and left his wad on the dresser at night. There were hundreds of dollars in loose cash. My mother had one regret. It bothered her the rest of her life. She never took any of the money.

MERCANTILE EXCHANGE

Ruby kept a seat on the Chicago Mercantile Exchange. He traded and lost in onions, potatoes, wife, and kids.

IN A RUSH

Ruby rented a place on the top floor of the Delaware Towers. His beat was Rush Street. He hung out at the Cloister Inn in the basement of the Maryland Hotel. He dropped a lot of money there. He could buy drinks for gangsters and their mistresses. But no matter how much he spent the bartender did not want to take a round with Ruby's two toddlers.

BROWNS

Ruby liked Browns underneath the "L" on South Wabash. It used to be the Wonder Bar, which used to be the 226 Club when it was one of Al Capone's joints. There was once a speakeasy in the back and a brothel upstairs.

The bartender kept a baseball bat by the booze. The meat was prime, the neighborhood not. Ruby dug into a hand-carved sandwich. We threw peanut shells on the floor.

Ruby parked in front of the Lexington Hotel, where King Alphonse and his crew used to hole up. The fourth floor was the inner sanctum. There was a "Room of Doom."

NEW CADILLAC

Ruby and Maury were partners in a gin game. One night they won big. Maury was wiser, more experienced. He worried that Ruby would blow his six thousand dollars. He took him to a car dealership. Ruby bought a red Cadillac. He drove it straight to Los Angeles.

THE FORMOSA CAFÉ

Ruby's girlfriend was a gangster's moll named Ann. Everyone but the gangster knew he followed her to the City of Angels. He was addicted to her body. They hung out at the Formosa Café in West Hollywood. In the 1940s Bugsy Siegel had a booth there with a safe embedded in the floor. He might have given a kickback to the place, or maybe he got one. Ruby loved it because you could still feel the mobster vibe.

SEPARATION ANXIETY

My parents separated when I was two years old. I don't remember living with my natural father, but my mom told me that when he moved out of the apartment, I broke into a rash all over my body. It lasted for days. He never came home. I never got over my allergies.

BEA'S TURN

Bernice Ginsburg was twenty years old when she married Robert Allweiss in the ballroom at the Belmont Hotel on Sheridan Road. It was not a big affair. But it was the one she wanted.

The newlyweds moved two doors away from Bob's parents on 71st Street on the South Side. Bea had found a second family. She was like a planet that had been pulled into another orbit.

DATING AGAIN

Ruby came back to Chicago with his tail between his legs. He moved in with Auntie Bea and Uncle Bob, who were newlyweds. My aunt idolized him as an older brother. My grandmother loved playing gin with him. They convinced my mother to give him another shot.

Ruby and Irma did not want to get divorced. They started dating again. It worked for a while. The cutups could always have fun. But Ruby was cavalier, Irma suspicious. They dated until they did not.

FIXING A SNACK

Ruby came home late one night. He went to the kitchen to fix a snack. The fridge was fuller than usual. He poured a glass of iced tea. It was sweet. At the table, things seemed slightly off. The cabinets were different. He realized he was in the wrong apartment. He rushed out in a panic. He forgot to flick off the light. He left the dirty dishes in the sink.

WHAT NOT TO DO

When he went to Los Angeles, Ruby turned over his business to Elaine's husband. But his brother-in-law wasn't a smelter. He didn't know what he was doing. In one year, he lost everything but the property. Ruby was bust. He sold the Cadillac. He partnered up with Maury. He started playing gin rummy full-time at the Sherman Hotel.

UNVERIFIABLE

My mom said Ruby lost the deed to Ellis Smelting in a game of gin.

A BAD CHEATER

Auntie Bea said that Ruby was a bad cheater because he was not good at keeping secrets. She also said that she would kill if anyone said anything bad about him.

TESTIMONY ACCORDING TO BEVERLY RUBENSTEIN

Ruby was in New York making a side deal on scrap aluminum. He had trouble breathing and went to Mount Sinai Hospital. He had a diaphragmatic hernia. Irma heard about it. She flew to LaGuardia Airport. When she walked into his hospital room, his girlfriend Ann was lying on the bed. Irma turned around and walked out. That was the end of it.

VERSION RECORDED BY ARLENE HIRSCH

Ruby made an airline reservation for Mr. and Mrs. Rubenstein. The airline called to confirm. Irma knew something suspicious was going on. She flew to New York. She took a cab to the Waldorf Astoria. She took an elevator to the twenty-third floor. Ruby answered the door. When she walked into his room, his girlfriend Pat was lying on the bed. Irma turned around and walked out. That was the end of it.

UNRELIABLE NARRATORS

Everyone involved in this story is an unreliable narrator. Lenie and I were too young to know what was going on. The adults were crazed. They weren't even adults.

ALL PARTIES CAN AGREE

Harold Rubenstein cheated on Irma Ginsburg Rubenstein. She found out. That was the end of it.

3

HOW IT BEGINS

I have an early memory of sitting at the kitchen table with my mother in the middle of the night. We are drinking warm milk. She is sad. I am trying to cheer her up with a funny story.

The world broke when my mother cried. I tried to fix it. This is how I invented the idea of tikkun olam—the world is broken, and someone needs to repair it.

I looked like my grandfather. My mom dressed me in suspenders like him too. I wore them over a short-sleeve button-down white shirt. They held up my blue jeans. I was her little old man.

ALTERNATE MASCULINITY

My grandfather gave me my first lesson in tenderness. He rolled up my sleeve and kissed me on the upper arm. That kiss made a lasting impression.

NIGHT MISSION

Lenie deployed a commando crawl on her secret mission to slip past my mother's bed to get to the chocolate drops in the crystal candy dish in the living room.

INAUGURATION DAY, 1953

Dwight D. Eisenhower was inaugurated, and the country celebrated my third birthday. The crowd chanted, "I like Ike, you like Ike, everybody likes Ike." But everyone did not like Ike. My grandfather was upset. He loved Adlai Stevenson instead. I chanted, "We don't like Ike, we don't like Ike."

THE FATHER FORMERLY KNOWN AS DADDY RUBY

At first, we called him *Daddy*. Then we called him *Daddy Ruby*. Then we didn't call him anything. Finally, we dropped *Daddy* altogether and called him *Ruby*.

ASTHMATIC CHILDHOOD

Thanks to the pot for boiling water that kept me leaning over the stove and inhaling steam that opened my lungs so I could breathe evenly again.

SECRETARIAL

After she separated from Ruby, my mother went back to work. She had five jobs in one year. She was pretty and charmed her way into secretary positions. She said it was because of her "cute" personality. But she didn't have any secretarial skills. She kept getting fired. Her last job stuck because she was moved over to receptionist. There she could cute it up all day with customers.

MOTHER DISTRACTED

My mother was working by day and dating at night. Lenie and I didn't see her much. We scarcely noticed because our grandmother was over.

My grandparents considered divorce a *shanda*—a shame, a scandal. It was an embarrassment for the family. They refused to live with us because they wanted my mom to remarry.

My grandmother arrived in the early morning. She put us to bed at night. But my mother was there when I woke up wheezing in darkness.

It was always just the two of us talking to each other late into the night.

NEXT TO GODLINESS

My grandmother remade the bed in her hotel room, so it looked as if no one had slept in it. She dusted the inside of lampshades. She leaned so far out of her apartment window to wipe it we worried she would fall into the street.

Anna was not a reader, but every week she dusted Oscar's books. She also dusted the cans on the kitchen shelves. She lined them up by height, like small soldiers. Their labels faced forward. They were ready for inspection.

My grandmother took two streetcars to get to our house in time for her elder daughter to go to work. She washed the day away. Whenever I said something dirty, she dragged me to the washroom and cleaned out my mouth with soap.

I shouted, "Shut up!" at Lenie. My grandmother considered this swearing and pulled me to the sink. Now when anyone says, "Shut up!" I remember the sour taste of Ivory soap.

My grandmother gave Lenie and me baths together. She was

a no-nonsense kind of scrubber. It was not a time for splashing around. The soap floated on the water, like a warning.

My grandmother was a pragmatist. Her philosophy was the truth. If I called someone a liar, she also pulled me to the kitchen sink.

IRMA PHILOSOPHICAL

Lenie and I collapsed in stitches on the floor. "If you're laughing now," my mother warned, "you'll be crying later."

Later, we started crying. "Cut it out," my mother said, "or I'll give you something to cry about."

―――――――

FIRST DAY OF KINDERGARTEN

I did not go gently into that good morning. They hauled me out of the front-hall closet kicking shoes and clutching raincoats.

It felt like a long walk to Cleveland, which was Grover Cleveland Elementary on Byron Street.

At recess, I stepped on a crack and broke my mother's back. No wonder she had spasms at night.

When my grandmother picked me up after school, I made a joke about throwing butter through a window to see a butterfly. She told me to stop throwing things.

RIDDLE

After I misbehaved at lunchtime, I made up a riddle:

Q: What's the most spoiled sandwich in kindergarten?

A: A bratwurst.

THE SIMPLE LIFE

I got sent home from school. "Life was a lot simpler when I was little," I told my grandmother.

She frowned: "Not really."

I asked my grandmother how she liked going to school when she was a girl. "You didn't like it or not like it," she said. "You went until you didn't go anymore."

My grandmother didn't know her birthday. Her daughters decided on January 1st. We banged it in with the new year.

A *simpleton* is someone who asks his grandmother how old she is.

We felt like movie stars when Grandma took us on a streetcar down Hollywood Avenue to Hollywood Park. We ate candy from Hollywood Bowl.

THE PEAR TREE

There was a pear tree in the next-door neighbor's yard. I got banned for bad behavior. My sister slipped in and tossed fat ones over the fence. She was left-handed. The pears skewed right. I snared them out of thin air.

CONFESSIONS

Just like St. Augustine I broke into the place with friends and stole some pears. They weren't even ripe. "I had no motive for wickedness except wickedness itself. It was foul, and I loved it."

SURREALISM ON THE FAR NORTH SIDE

Don lived on Wayne Street, my favorite dead end, where there was a house that had a garage door without a garage. You lifted it up and stepped into an overgrown yard.

Don's parents said, "Go play on the Prairie." They meant a vacant lot over by Maplewood. It had giant flying grasshoppers that flew over the bricks and broken glass. We left them alone because they spewed brown stuff when you swatted them.

One day I came home with a stop sign that I found in the dirt, but my grandmother made me put it back. I propped it up where it should go.

The Irving Park Villa put the park in Irving Park, but we liked our own meadow better—even if it didn't have grass.

Don's friend Jerry got fireworks from his dad's account at the corner tavern. He liked to play with matches and lighter fluid. One day he burned down the Prairie. I didn't get to see it, though, because by then we had moved away.

MY FIRST MOVIE

was a religious service. The Sheridan Theatre on Irving Park Road had recently been converted into a synagogue. The blowing of the shofar was the show. There were apples with honey.

A DIAGONAL INCISION

The new Northwest Expressway cut right through the heart of the old neighborhood. It was like bypass surgery. It got blood flowing to the northern suburbs.

After President Kennedy was assassinated in 1963, the Northwest Expressway was renamed the Kennedy Expressway. It became the road to Camelot.

FREUDIAN SLIPS

None of us had heard of Johann Wolfgang von Goethe, the wizard of Weimar. We called it *Go-thee Street*.

A stop on the Irving Park bus was pronounced *Moat-Zart*.

Nobody had been to Devon, England, so we pronounced it *de-Vahn Avenue*.

My Auntie Bea was irritated that Berenice Avenue was called

Bare-uh-niece. She didn't mind that Bryn Mawr Avenue was called *Brin-mar.*

It was annoying when people pronounced our state *Ill-i-noise.*

My friend Johnny used to live on Freud Street in Detroit. Everyone called it *Frood.* He needed therapy.

RED-LETTER DAY

I was learning to ride a blue two-wheeler. My mother learned to ride a red bicycle in just one afternoon. I wondered if a blue bike would have taken her a whole day.

STORY TIME

It's time to put your head down on the desk for story time. It's time to clean out your locker. It's time to file into the schoolyard for a fire drill. It's time to pull on a sleek yellow slicker and splash home in the rain. It's time to throw your arms around your grandmother's neck. It's time to dunk sugar cookies in milk. It's time to play in a fort next to your bed. It's time to remember a time before you knew about time.

―――――

A NEW GIRLFRIEND

Ruby's new girlfriend was tall and danced mambo cha-cha in Latino clubs. Olé, it was a Jewish craze. She loved an underground spot called the Marble Stairway on Michigan Avenue. That's where they met.

Ruby introduced us in the park. We hit the swings and teeter-totters. She was light on her feet.

My mother knew Ruby's girlfriend from the old neighborhood. Her father, Tevele, was a well-known cantor at Congregation Beth Itzchok. Her brother, Jordan, was a cantor at Synagogue Beth El. They could lift the rooftops with their voices.

Beverly Cohen could chant the prayers too. She was a good Jewish girl. My mother no longer thought so.

THE WALLS HAVE EARS

My mom shared her suspicion with my aunt. She was put out that Beverly was putting out.

A VOLATILE REDHEAD

Uncle Ben was a volatile redhead. He was Beverly's mentor, her moral compass. He espoused ethics.

Ruby knew Ben from the scrap business. They went to conventions in Springfield together. There were risqué parties at those conventions. Ruby knew about Ben's taste for hookers.

After Ruby met Beverly, he telephoned Ben to say he was going to marry his favorite niece. Ruby teased him. "Poor Beverly is going to know everything about you now."

The call was a success. Ben went nuts.

NOGOODNIK

Uncle Ben campaigned against Ruby. He would never let Beverly marry a person like that. He knew what he was talking about. Ruby was a nogoodnik. Beverly didn't know what to say. She couldn't argue he was a goodnik.

WHO CARES?

Beverly's mother wanted Beverly to get married. She didn't need a spinster on her hands. Ruby was Jewish. That was good enough for her. She didn't care about his character. You can always get a character. You can't always get a husband.

EITHER / OR

Beverly's grandmother Fanny Feingold was ready to open her purse and celebrate. She had a policy of bringing two checks to weddings. If she liked where she was sitting, she gave the bride and groom a generous gift. If she didn't like her table, she gave them a measly amount. The account was full, but the checks were still blank.

A GET

Out of sheer spite, Ruby refused to grant my mother an official Jewish divorce. But Beverly came from an Orthodox Jewish family. She would never marry Ruby until he got religious clearance. Harold and Irma went to an ecclesiastical court. They severed souls. Ruby handed over the document. The marriage was dissolved. My mother got her Get.

A HEDONIST

Ruby was trying to discourage Beverly from marrying him. He confessed to being a hedonist. Beverly had never heard the word before. It had something to do with living for pleasure. What's wrong with that? She liked pleasure.

Ruby leaned forward with intensity. Beverly was not getting the message. He was not marriage material. He looked into her eyes. He told her his motto: *Eat, Fuck, Suck*.

Beverly was stunned by Ruby's pronouncement. She had to hand it to him, though. He showed courage by telling her the truth. You had to love a guy with guts. They could date. Maybe they should hold off on the wedding.

————

BLOOD AND PEE

"Blood ain't pee," Ruby said. This was one of his favorite maxims. I didn't understand it. But I checked the color when I went to the bathroom. Pee ain't blood either.

THREE UNCLES

Ruby told us about his three favorite uncles. These were Bubb's boys, his grandmother's brothers.

Uncle Morris drove a bus and parked it on the side street in front of Ruby's house. That was cool.

Uncle Itchy was a henchman for the union. He was a bigshot, who scared people for a living. That was even cooler.

Uncle Sammy got caught with his hand in the till and had to do eighteen months in a low-security prison. That was not cool. But the prison was like a country club. When he got out, he was rich. That was the coolest thing of all.

AUNTIE AYA

Like his mom's sister, Ruby didn't mind causing a scandal. Aya was a flapper. She married a French-horn player in Victor Young's Orchestra and moved to Los Angeles. He was grub. She had verve. Until she got MS, Auntie Aya could really cut the rug at bar mitzvahs and weddings.

AUNTS AND UNCLES

Ruby and Irma had a tight group of friends from school. My mother made us call each of them aunt and uncle. They paired up early: Aunt Edie and Uncle Snooky, Aunt Idel and Uncle Shelly, Aunt Phyllis and Uncle Solly. She added new fake relatives to the group, too, like Aunt Harriet and Uncle Al or Aunt Norma and Uncle Sy or Aunt Edie and Uncle Jackie. They were not Darwinians, but they had the stuff. The women were loud, the men shady, and the parties raucous. As a result, we felt we had a large family of nut jobs.

THE MENTALITY

They grew up during the Depression without money. They thought of themselves as middle-class. Everyone worked. Their morals were flexible. No one had a job—everyone had a hustle.

ON THE SIDE

I went to a restaurant with four of my uncles. There was a lot of joshing—deals were getting cut. "What's a tenth-of-a-cent a pound to you?" "What's an extra bolt of cloth?" When the waiter came, no one wanted a main course. Everyone ordered sides.

SOME ADVICE

Aunt Idel, Aunt Edie, Aunt Harriet, and my mom can carry on at a restaurant. The mood is festive, the noise level high. It's going to get brassy. If you're sitting nearby, you're welcome to join in the hilarity. But if you want to talk to each other, you might want to change tables.

SPLITTING DESSERT

Everyone is full. No one wants to split dessert with Aunt Idel. She looks over at the next table. "Would anyone like to split a piece of apple strudel?"

VOLUME CONTROL

My mom could project, but Aunt Idel really cranked up the volume. The only other woman in her stratosphere was Aunt Harriet.

In the low-volume department, Uncle Shelly didn't say much,

but he was no match for Uncle Al, who only mumbled. Al was so quiet my mom thought he was refined.

Uncle Al and Aunt Harriet owned a children's clothing store. Al was the only one in their crowd who graduated from college, Northwestern no less. My mom mentioned it all the time. It was like a merit badge he wore to parties.

I wondered if Uncle Al was that smart, though, because he married You-Know-Who, who bossed him around all day at work and then kept it up at home.

SECRET COUNCILS

The Women of the Secret Council met at the kitchen table and spoke Yiddish so the kids wouldn't understand. The Children of the Secret Council met in a fort in the yard and spoke Igpay Atinlay.

THE EMERGENCY

We were in the yard with the pear tree. Roberta was brandishing a broom. She threatened to hit Lenie. I stepped forward to stop this from happening. Roberta slammed the broom handle down on my head. Suddenly, there was blood everywhere. I ran home clutching my skull and screaming: "My brains are falling out! My brains are falling out!"

My grandmother was calm. She gathered her purse, took Lenie and me by the hand, and went out to the street to catch a cab to the hospital. One pulled over immediately.

"You don't have the brains you were born with," she said dryly, settling down in the back seat. "I don't think you have to worry that anything is going to start falling out now."

SWAN DIVE

I jumped up and down on my bed. The bed made a good trampoline. I could soar high. One afternoon I lost control and took a swan dive onto the floor. My forehead was spurting blood. My grandmother was imperturbable. She hailed a cab. They remembered us in the emergency room. They stitched me up, like a veteran. I still didn't have the brains I was born with.

BRAIN SALE

"If we sold everyone's brains," my grandmother said to me, "I'd charge the most for yours."

"Why, because I'm the smartest one in the family?"

"No, because yours have never been used."

4

THE SLEEPWALKER

I walked through the hallway in a trance. I climbed down the stairs and opened the front door. It was snowing. My mother closed it gently and guided me back to bed. I did not wake up. The next day she bought me warmer pajamas.

A SMALL MISTAKE

My mother was sitting in the living room with a man. He introduced himself, "I'm Kurt. That's Kurt with a K."

K had started showing up a lot. We didn't see the point.

One night I drifted into the living room in my sleep. I mistook K for the urinal. I peed on his leg. My mother steered me back to bed.

K didn't show up for at least a month. My mom thought it was over. Mission accomplished!

OGAY AWAYWAY!

Uncle Kurt was back. This called for a special meeting of the Secret Council. We might have to send a warning: *Ogay awayway!*

THE UNCONSCIOUS

My mom was having coffee with K in the kitchen. I drifted over in my sleep. I opened the door to the kitchen closet. It looked like a urinal. I peed on the floor. My mother walked me back to bed. K did not walk out. He had made up his mind. Mission failure!

THE PICK CONGRESS

My mom said that she met Kurt at the Glass Hat bar in the Ambassador Hotel. This was almost true. She met him at the Glass Hat cabaret in the Pick Congress Hotel. She didn't like to admit she liked it there. It was a pickup joint. There was a suave guy on the glass dance floor. He spotted her across the room. He asked her to dance.

COURTSHIP

Kurt was handsome. He had blue eyes and movie-star looks. Irma could overlook that he was too short. She was twenty-eight. He said he was thirty-eight. She thought he was mature because he was balding. She was flirtatious, but she had very little experience. She'd never been anywhere. He drove a blue convertible. He had adventures with women. He knew how to order a cocktail. He was dashing and liked to dance.

THE OLD DAYS

We spied them clutching in the kitchen. Then Kurt ran out of the house. He was flustered. We didn't know why. Why was because Irma didn't believe in sex before marriage.

UNFORGIVING

Kurt was a forty-five-year-old bachelor. He had been married for a short time a long time ago. He married a dancer named Pearl and promptly enlisted in the navy.

He sailed off the way sailors do. They were both at sea. During the war, she divorced him.

Kurt moved back in with his widowed mother. She liked living with her eldest son. She did not approve of a younger divorcee with two children. She opposed the marriage.

My mother never forgave her. Irma was Old Testament. Everyone knew that it was not a good idea to cross her. Five years later, when my dad asked if his mother could live with us, my mom refused. He was forced to place her in a nursing home. He yelled at us every time he visited her on the South Side.

Pearl once called my dad to see what he was doing. What he was doing was sitting at the kitchen table with my mom. The conversation was strangled.

IN THE DARK

My mom didn't warn us she was getting married. We weren't invited to the wedding. She tied the knot in a rabbi's study. Then she left for their honeymoon.

HONEYMOON IN FLORIDA

I have a photograph of them on their honeymoon in Miami Beach. They look like Alan Ladd and Elizabeth Taylor. My mother has jet-black hair and red lipstick. She is wearing a pale pants suit and dangling a cigarette from two fingers. Kurt has thick black glasses. He is wearing white slacks and a button-down fishnet short-sleeve shirt. They are sitting at an outdoor bar at the Fontainebleau Hotel. He has his left hand on her right knee. They seem conscious of cutting a figure, posing for a photo, living it up with style.

THE FATHER FORMERLY KNOWN AS UNCLE KURT

Uncle Kurt moved in with us. We figured out they had gotten married when our mom told us to start calling him *Daddy Kurt*. We said, "Is that Kurt with a K?" But we didn't call him anything for months.

MAMA'S BOY

Kurt thought I was too much of a mama's boy. He decided to get me interested in sports. One day he was standing behind me while I was hitting in a batting cage. The mechanical robot threw, and I connected on a hard line drive. Kurt said, "Good hit. That would be a double."

I turned around and said, "Thanks, Dad." It startled both of us.

He said, "Concentrate on the pitch. Let's turn up the speed on the next one."

THE SWITCH

Lenie and I started calling Kurt *Dad* when Ruby wasn't around. We wondered if we should start calling Ruby *Uncle Harold*.

———

INHERITANCE

When Kurt became my father, his parents became my grandparents. I adopted them as my own. Their history became my history, too.

TWO SONS

My grandparents Otto and Selma Hirsch had two sons, Kurt Siegfried and Hans Gottlieb. Hans had curly red hair that looked like a burning bush. He was pudgy and needed protection. Kurt was a stutterer. He was small and did the protecting. It was not easy to be either of them. There was no mental-health perspective.

A COUNTRY / CITY MARRIAGE

Kurt was born in Mannheim, Germany. His mother came from the village of Enkirch, on the Moselle River; his father was a Mannheimer. She had a kitchen garden. He had a large map of town. She went barefoot, he wore boots.

A RAILROAD CONDUCTOR

Otto was a railroad conductor on a trolley that circled Square City. Every day Kurt raced through a sugar beet field to bring him his lunch pail. Otto checked his watch to make sure that his son arrived on time. The train was never late. Otto tipped his hat. He shouted, *"Alle an Bord!"* and blew his whistle. The father pulled out. The son beat it home through the sweet beets.

A GUARD IN WORLD WAR I

After he was shot down in a fighter plane, Kurt's father was deployed to guard French prisoners in a small village. Kurt could remember how he marched them by the house and snuck them in for tea. My grandmother made him keep his rifle in the hall. The prisoners sang sad French songs and gave the boys chewing gum because they missed their families.

IMMIGRATION

After World War I, Otto had a premonition about the Nazis and followed his cousins to Chicago. He worked as a spotter in the back of a dry cleaner. He felt fortunate to escape the Germans. But his cousins treated him badly and he hated his job.

NEAR WEST

Otto and Selma settled on the Near West Side of Chicago. No one in the family spoke English. They were the only Jews in the neighborhood.

Every afternoon Kurt Siegfried and Hans Gottlieb were jumped on their way home from school. Kurt was a scrapper. After his parents went to bed, he climbed out the bedroom window to track down his enemies and finish the fight.

NEW AMERICANS

The family became American citizens. Kurt dropped Siegfried. Hans Gottlieb changed his name to Harry George.

BAD ACTORS

My dad's dad loved professional wrestling. The atmosphere reminded him of Germany in the early 1920s. He had an eye for bad actors. He thought some of the matches were rigged, others were real.

LITTLE ITALY

My dad liked to return to his old neighborhood. We learned about Halsted and Taylor Streets because he knew the best place for an Italian beef sandwich, an Italian lemonade, and a cannoli.

STEPGRANDPARENTS

Grandpa Hirsch died before I was born. I remember Grandma Hirsch reaching down and touching her toes in the Drexel Home for the Aged. She was stocky and spry. She clutched her purse to her chest. She thought the staff was stealing from her. My parents said she was senile.

HATRED OF GERMANY

I never heard my father speak a word of German. He spoke English without any trace of an accent. He would not drink Fanta and cursed Volkswagen Beetles. He hated everything about Germany except the music of Richard Strauss, which he listened to religiously, and the food, which he loved. We went to Little Heidelberg for his birthday. He ordered sauerkraut soup and Wiener schnitzel.

WHAT KIND OF NAME IS HIRSCH ANYWAY?

I had to find out for myself that the surname *Hirsch* means "deer" in German. We probably came from a family of foresters. My dad did not want to hunt, but he wouldn't be hunted either.

BOXING IT UP

Our new dad was a box salesman. For a price, he measured and boxed up anything anyone needed. He could contain everything but his temper.

Kurt learned to box in the navy. He had been a lightweight contender in the Golden Gloves. Quick and compact, he could dodge and jab. But he got knocked silly in the fifth round of a championship bout. He quit boxing. He did not quit fighting.

An aircraft mechanic on the USS *Enterprise,* Kurt worked on scout planes, dive bombers, and Wildcat fighters. He prepared them for war.

Kurt was a sprinter. I still have his tarnished track-and-field medal from the YMCA in 1932. I keep it on my bookshelf to remember how fast he had to run.

Kurt saw Crazy Legs Hirsch play halfback for the Chicago Rockets in 1948. He was bowlegged and could imitate Elroy's twisted running style. "The way I grew up," he said, "you learned to be shifty."

Kurt was a wrestler. He had competed at the West Side Y. His specialty was cutting your feet out from under you. One moment you were standing next to him, the next you were not.

We laid it down on the grass. Kurt could get you into a hold. Wrestling is so tiring! After two minutes, you're ready to cry *Uncle.* You need to get pinned to cry *Dad.*

———————

Mr. and Mrs. O'Malley kept a plaster Jesus on the dashboard of their car. He had tears in his eyes. People probably converted just to cheer him up.

My neighbor Christian always arrived with good news.

Buddig ham cost nineteen cents a package. Even we knew that it didn't taste like real ham.

I asked my grandmother if it was kosher to mix a meat product, like Buddig turkey, with a cheese product, like Velveeta. She said, "Why would you want to eat that?"

Our first Christmas! My mother hung stockings on the fireplace. She understood that Jews are not supposed to unwrap presents under a pine tree on Christmas morning, but she did not want to be left out of the fun. It wasn't fair. Why should Christmas have anything to do with the birth of Christ?

Poor Santa Claus has a lot to do on Christmas Eve. He must have been in a rush, because he forgot his snack by the fireplace. We could see our mom sneaking his cookies. She dunked them in his milk.

The Santa on State Street never came through. Who wants school clothes for Christmas? The packaging was merry, the presents not.

Who needs another coloring book of Rudolph the Red-Nosed Reindeer? Montgomery Ward was giving them out for free.

Not everyone knows that Robert May, who created Rudolph, used the proceeds to buy a house in Skokie. We drove down his block to look at Christmas lights.

Bing Crosby was so dreamy singing "White Christmas" that you could forget the song was written by a Russian Jew. Or else you could boast about it.

The only Jewish thing we did on Christmas was to eat Chinese food and watch movies.

Our mother made us kneel next to our beds at night. She didn't care that Jews don't kneel anymore. She told us to recite, "Now I lay me down to sleep." At the end, we were supposed to say, "God bless Mom, God bless Dad," and God bless anyone else we wanted to make it through the night. She warned us not to leave anyone out or they might die overnight. We worried it would be our fault. We got so tired going through all the names we crawled into bed and fell asleep.

THE ALMIGHTY INSANE

The Almighty Insane Popes Nation was a greaser gang that staked out Kilbourn Park. They were Greek to me. Maybe it was happenstance, but we left the neighborhood and the Popes moved in.

GO NORTH

Northward, ho! It's time for a new start for a new family. We're packing the wagons for a two-mile trek. Goodbye, Irving! We're moving to North Park.

FOLLOWING MARTIN KIMBELL

My family had never heard of Martin Kimbell. But he was our man!

Kimbell traveled from upstate New York in 1836 to claim 160 acres of midwestern prairie. He rejected land at Dearborn and Lake as "a damned mudhole." The slough was too close to the Chicago River. He didn't like the lakefront either. If he was going to succeed in Mud City, he preferred a dry field five miles northwest where he could plant hay and make it.

The Kimbell farm was centered at the corner of what is now Milwaukee, Kimball, and Diversey. My dad drove by and called it "suicide corner." He was an erratic driver. I thought we should take another route.

Other settlers followed to towns called Jefferson, Maplewood, and Avondale. In 1889, they combined into Logan Square, which was named after a Union army general. In the 1930s, my grandparents, the Ginsburgs, settled there with two daughters.

My family did not call the neighborhood Bucktown. That was a name for goats. Logan Square had a boulevard system which started with the World's Fair. Streetcars ruled. The elevated train station was the end of the line.

Everyone looked up at a seventy-foot marble column topped by an eagle. It's a monument to statehood designed by the same architect as the Lincoln Memorial. Thank you, Henry Bacon. Chicago has people at the base. Washington has a temple.

The neighborhood gathered to honor the war dead. The veterans wore uniforms. There were speeches. No one remembered

General John A. Logan, who founded Memorial Day. His statue is on a mound in Grant Park.

There are no monuments for brewers or landowners. The city decided to honor Michael Diversy by naming an avenue after him. But some doofus official misspelled his name as Diversey. The city also honored Martin Kimbell with a street. His name was misspelled as Kimball.

The Diversy family may not have cared—they had beer to sell—but the Kimbell clan did. The error infuriated Martin's son Charles. He was a proto-modernist with a horse and wagon. He used a paintbrush to change the letter *a* to the letter *e* on all the street signs.

The city responded as cities do. It repainted the signs with the wrong spelling.

In 1956, my parents settled at 5716 N. Kimball Avenue.

THE HOUSE ON KIMBALL

My parents found a red ranch house smack-dab in the middle of a block of three-flats. They were taller, but we could spread out.

The backyard looked like a narrow baseball diamond. The goal was to hit one that soared over the apple tree, the red fence, and the wooden door to the alley.

My grandparents liked the new house. "This is America," my grandfather said. "No one is above or below us."

My grandmother tut-tutted. "They're renting. There's a landlord."

KIDS PLAY

Lenie and I hit the alley together. There was a Wiffle ball game going on. It was like a running craps game. The school playground was also our beat. We played with boys and girls. We didn't distinguish so long as the girls were tomboys.

We lived between Swedish evangelicals and Orthodox Jews. They were always trying to convert one another. I tried to convert them too—to baseball. But I could never convince them to play pickup with us.

Our neighborhood was named after North Park Theological Seminary on Foster Avenue. The campus was like church: no fun.

Our parents threatened to send us to the Chicago Parental School when we misbehaved. But the scare didn't work, because the school had a farm with animals and a cool-looking playground. We liked the idea of joining the truants.

It looked like a giant nature preserve, but it wasn't worth getting TB just to be admitted to the sanitarium on Bryn Mawr and Crawford.

We challenged each other to run through the Bohemian National Cemetery on North Pulaski Road. There were lots of dead Czech people around. The live ones moved out of North Park long ago.

Mayor Cermak took a bullet for president-elect Roosevelt. He was buried there for good.

Our dad measured our heights. We had already outgrown Chicago's only waterfall. Dammed, it was four feet tall.

RUNNING AWAY

My mother and I had an argument. I decided to leave home. She helped me pack a suitcase. I did not tell her where I was going. She assumed I would walk around and come back, but by the late afternoon she started to worry. By nightfall, she was frantic. She began calling my friends. She tracked me down at Gary O'Neil's house. On the phone, she sounded irritated and amused. I wanted to stay the weekend, but Gary's mother made me go home.

THE WIFFLE BALL KID

Gary's father was a janitor who picked up lost Wiffle balls from the gutters and rooftops. We played stick ball in the alley. Once you hit one up there, it was hard to retrieve. That's why the Wiffle Ball Kid had so much cred in the neighborhood.

"A HOT TIME IN THE OLD TOWN"

I sang:

Late last night when we were all in bed
Old Lady Leary left a lantern in the shed.
The cow kicked it over, and this is what they said:
"There'll be a hot time in the old town tonight!"

Gary said Mrs. O'Leary's cow didn't really start the Chicago Fire in 1871. His dad told him it was just a way to blame Irish immigrants. After that, I didn't sing the words anymore.

I liked to skip around the block. Sometimes I forgot and hummed the tune to myself.

WHAT A YO-YO!

I couldn't manage the tricks. The sleeper woke up. The dog ran away when I walked it. I could only make it halfway around the world.

TIDDLYWINKS

Don't play tiddlywinks with grown-ups. They are simpletons who wink, drink, and slur words, like *squidgers* and *squopping*. It sounds like drunken babytalk.

THE TOOTH FAIRY

Our tooth fairy was cheap. We got a quarter. Myron's tooth fairy was generous. He got twenty bucks because his mom pulled the wrong bill out of her wallet in the dark.

I wrapped my bloody tooth in a white hankie and showed it to Ruby. He cringed. But he gave me a five-dollar bill for luck.

WHY WE DIDN'T SEE BEVERLY ANYMORE

Ann came back to Chicago. Ruby went dark on Beverly. Today they call it *ghosting*. But a gangster's moll goes back to her gangster. Ruby was left high and dry. He went fishing on the pier. Beverly didn't bite.

THE MANICURIST

Pat was a manicurist at the Palmer House in downtown Chicago. Ruby loved manicures. Pat had a side hustle at the hotel. Ruby loved a good side hustle. He said, "I love Pat because she is gentle with me."

BIG HERM'S

We were standing in line for a hotdog at Big Herm's. Ruby said, "Women like me because I have a small penis."

A NEW WIFE

Ruby took us to Libertyville on a Saturday visitation. It was a long drive through the country. We listened to doo-wop on the radio. We were going to meet his new wife, Patricia, and her teenage son, Bucky, our new stepbrother.

Bucky led my sister to the yard and exposed himself. Lenie ran away.

Pat had long hair and wore high heels in the kitchen. It smelled of oatmeal and perfume. She was older and sexier than our mother.

"She's not his wife," our mom said when we got home. "She's a prostitute."

We didn't know the meaning of the word. "That's a woman your father pays to touch him," she explained. "You can't see her anymore."

Then she picked up the phone.

WHAT'S A PROSTITUTE?

"I bet you don't know what a prostitute is," I told the kids on the playground. No one knew. I said, "That's a woman my dad pays to do stuff to him."

———

IT'S ELEMENTARY

I protested that I was innocent, but the trial was over. There was no appeal. The convict was required to report for second grade to the penitentiary Peterson Elementary School.

The Petersons owned lots of land in North Park. Mary Gage Peterson was a conservationist who donated some of this land to build a school that looked like a prison house.

Peher Peterson was a pioneering nursery man who transplanted trees all over the city. A huge chunk of his leafy land became a TB sanitarium that became North Park Village. His wife wrote "Nature Lover's Creed" ("I believe in nature, and in God's out-of-doors . . ."). It didn't say anything about bars on the windows of school buildings.

The school opened on Christiana Avenue in 1926. I drove by it recently. It has been refurbished. What I recall as a jail is now a handsome redbrick building.

GOING NUCLEAR

The Soviets tested a nuclear bomb four months before I was born. We grew up together. The "existential threat" was like a school bully. The school was so scared of him that it sounded a loud siren. When summer ended, we practiced hiding under our desks. Our teachers called it "duck and cover."

BEDRIDDEN

Lenie reported for one day of first grade. Then she came down with strep throat. She had to stay home. No one paid attention until it turned into scarlet fever. She was rushed to the hospital. It morphed into nephritis.

Ruby said he did not like hospitals and never visited. But he sent Lenie a TV set. She liked the gift because it reminded her that he was out there somewhere. She could pretend he was watching over her when she watched a show.

My mother was enraged because Ruby did not help pay the bills. Kurt footed everything. She worried he would dump us. He did not. He carried Lenie from the hospital to the car to the house.

Lenie went to her room and turned on *Kukla, Fran and Ollie*. The show lasted fifteen minutes. She stayed in bed for fourteen months.

SKIRMISH ON THE PAJAMA FIELD

On the night Lenie was rushed to the hospital, my aunt grabbed a pair of pajamas for me and tossed them into an overnight bag. At her house, I did not want to put on girl's pajamas. Bea was in no mood for my lip. She slapped me hard across the face. I wore what I was told.

BOXES OF CARDS

Aunt Edie put an ad in the paper saying that a sick girl would like to receive mail. Letters flooded in. Lenie didn't feel well enough to respond. My mom stacked thousands of cards in boxes. When we moved to Skokie, she stacked the boxes in the basement. The basement flooded.

MEDIEVAL WARFARE

Larry Hockwood was the neighborhood bully. He patrolled the alley between our houses. He tossed stones over the fence at the Wiffle Ball Kid and me. We fired crabapples at him. We landed some too. Lenie sat in a box seat on the porch and rooted for the home team.

BACK-ALLEY ANTI-SEMITISM

The insult flew over my head. Why would someone call me a kite?

THE GOLDFISH VARIATIONS

1.

London gave Lenie a goldfish in a bowl for her birthday. She forgot to poke breathing holes in the paper. The gift was dead in the water.

2.

I won a goldfish at the school fair. My mom held the goldfish in her left hand while she cleaned the bowl with her right. Her hand broke out in a rash. The goldfish survived another day.

3.

Our cousin Mickey slept over. He eyed the goldfish in the bowl. He cupped it in his hands. He swallowed it.

4.

Goldfish can live up to ten years. In our house, they were lucky to make it ten days.

5.

There were years when we lived with an empty goldfish bowl.

U

There were thirty-five kids in my class. We were clamped into our seats. Generations of inmates had carved their initials into the wooden desks. The desks were screwed to the floor.

My scrawl was poor in pen and pencil. Mrs. Movehill, my favorite teacher, gave me a U in penmanship. That was Unsatisfactory.

"If you don't do better," she warned, "no one will read your writing."

BLACK RHINOCEROS

The black rhinoceros at Brookfield Zoo eating sweet potatoes, carrots, and bread looked like my extended family crowding around the table at Thanksgiving.

Mrs. Movehill said that the black rhino is the same muddy color as the white rhino, which is strange if you think about it, and we did.

Rhinos have poor eyesight and swivel their tube-shaped ears in all directions so they can hear their enemies approaching, lions and people who carve their horns into daggers or mash them into pain relievers.

What does it feel like to have two horns tilting up on a huge head, Mr. Rhinoceros?

You lumber around in your skin of armor like an exiled general.

You're the closest thing I've ever seen to a grounded unicorn.

A pachyderm in peril would still rather live in an open savannah.

ACCORDION LESSONS

After she went to a polka dance, my mother decided that I should learn to play accordion. I tried. Every good boy does not do fine. The accordion was bigger than me. I never got past the bass buttons or figured out the bellows. I quit the lessons quicker than you can squeeze a chord.

BUBBLES IN THE WINE

My grandmother watched Lawrence Welk on Saturday night at 8 p.m. She considered him the greatest accordion player who ever lived.

PRACTICE FOR LIFE

My mother's friend Mel was my Peewee League baseball manager. He outshined everyone else in the league because he had been a minor league catcher. That's how he snagged Aunt Mary, too.

Uncle Mel didn't want his son Jeff or me to be afraid of the ball, which is why he dusted us off during batting practice. He aimed at our knees and threw at our shoulders. He tried to bean us. We scrambled to the dirt to avoid getting hit.

Uncle Mel said that being a catcher was the quickest way to the big leagues, so we strapped on leg guards, chest protectors, and masks. We were field commanders gearing up for battle.

Uncle Mel taught us to plant ourselves and block the plate. We took turns sliding into home and tagging each other out.

Our manager hit popups into the sun. We dropped our masks and tried catching them. Sometimes they caught us. I got plonked a few times.

On the mound, Uncle Mel was wild. He fired fastballs over our heads and snapped sinkers at our feet.

Uncle Mel was the Zen master of Peewee League. He said, "Pay attention. Nothing should get past you."

6

ONE DAY IN SEPTEMBER

Our mom came home with a new baby. Lenie and I hadn't noticed she was pregnant.

SURPRISE!

My dad was surprised when my mom got pregnant. My mom was not surprised. It was intentional. But it was her intention. My dad's inattention was his greatest joy.

N IS CLOSE TO O

Does proximity count? Nancy was named after my dad's father, Otto. My mom didn't like any girls' names beginning with the letter *O* and so she moved up the alphabet to the letter *N*.

My mom's father was still alive. After he died, she doubled up and said Nancy was named after Oscar, too.

Lenie and I decided that Nancy could have been named Opal because she was a gem.

"IF YOU PRICK US, DO WE NOT BLEED?"

Everyone huddled around the crib. Nancy was not crying. We thought she was fine. My mom thought something was wrong. She stuck Nancy with a safety pin. That was not safe. Nancy bled. Nancy cried.

CRYING IN THE CRIB

Nancy was a sympathetic baby. She cried alone in her crib while my mom cried to her friends on the phone.

Nancy was not a sympathetic baby. She cried alone in her crib while my mom laughed with her friends on the phone.

TEARS, IDLE TEARS

Whenever Nancy tells the story of the crib, she jokes that she's been crying ever since. Then she tears up.

DOLL IN THE HOUSE

1.

Auntie Bea said that my mom didn't realize that Nancy was a real person until she became a teenager. Until then, she thought Nancy was a perfect little doll.

2.

I didn't play with dolls, but this one was fun. You could bounce her up and down like Silly Putty. She made weird gurgling noises. Her burps were loud. She got smelly, but your parents had to deal with that. Your mom didn't want you to sling her over your shoulder. You got away with it when no one was looking.

HOT IRON

My dad was babysitting for Lenie and Nancy. He had Nancy in his arms when he dropped a hot iron. He called the fire department. The truck arrived with great fanfare. Three men tromped into the house. My dad said, "What should I do?"

The fireman said, "Pick it up."

My dad replied, "My hands are full here."

The fireman said, "Hand me the baby."

PROHIBITION AGAINST NURSING

After her illness, Lenie said that she wanted to be a nurse. My mom told her that Jewish girls can't become nurses.

Poor Deborah, the wet nurse of Rebecca, who was Jacob's mother. If it were up to my mom, she never would have made it into Genesis.

ROBBERY

We came home late one night. The front door was flapping open. Our house had been robbed. But the thieves only took three things: jewelry, silverware, and Lenie's TV. They all came from Ruby. The robbers were no fools. There was nothing else worth stealing.

———

BROWN COWS

For a treat, Grandma made her famous brown cows. The vanilla ice cream floated through the foam on top of the root beer. The cows looked spotted.

PENNY CANDY

Lenie and I were back together in the schoolyard. At the penny-candy store across the street from Peterson, we bought colorful buttons stuck on wax paper. The storekeeper threw in bloopers for free. The pink ones had bled red. The blue ones bruised purple.

We tore off the cellophane and smoked red licorice pipes. We blew strawberry smoke rings into each other's mouths.

The only gold we ever touched was the wrapping on chocolate gold coins.

We had little inanimate pet gummy worms and bears that we ate.

I popped an Atomic FireBall and shouted, "My mouth is on fire!" The flame lasted a few seconds. Then I popped another. The fire raged.

We couldn't afford an entire pack of candy cigarettes. Like hoodlums, we bummed them one at a time in the schoolyard.

Nik-L-Nips cost a nickel. You bit the cap, slurped the syrup, and popped the bottle into your mouth like chewing tobacco. Then you staggered around acting drunk. Prohibition was over. You had blown your wad.

SPIT IN YOUR HAND

If you *really* want to make a deal, spit in your hand, and shake on it.

GUYS AND DOLLS

For Halloween, the boys dressed up as hoodlums and gangsters, big shots with toy machine guns and pink candy cigars. The girls dressed up as dames and floozies.

My mom objected. She wanted me to dress up as "a big-time lawyer." She wanted Lenie to be "a pretty lady." I dressed as a mob lawyer. Lenie dressed as a gangster gal.

After trick-or-treating, my mom picked through our loot and confiscated the chocolate bars for herself. We were left with lollipops and candy corn. But gangsters do not cry. They get even. We bided our time and stole them back.

GANGSTER GAMES

"I'll be John Dillinger," someone shouted on the playground.

"That's not fair. You got to be Dillinger last time."

"Okay, I'll be Machine Gun McGurn."

RUNNING WILD

Lenie and I were running wild in the house. The new babysitter was old. She was sleeping on the couch downstairs. We checked on her now and then. She was taking it easy. We went crazy for the whole night. We had never had such a lenient sitter. Uncle Sy and Aunt Norma drove by the house. They wondered why all the doors were open. Our parents came home. The babysitter had suffered a stroke. She died on the couch.

NO TRIAL

We felt terrible about the babysitter's death. We waited to be put in handcuffs. No one came to arrest us. No one hauled us down to the station for interrogation. There was no test, no arraignment, no trial. Where were the gumshoes? Where were the reporters? Chicago justice wasn't what it was cracked up to be. The only consequence was that we had a new babysitter. She was a teenager.

THIS BABYSITTER SHALL REMAIN NAMELESS

We never knew our babysitters. They didn't come around much. My mother didn't like paying for someone to watch us. She'd rather mooch off our grandparents. I've always felt bad about the babysitter who died. We drew a blank for her name.

———

WEDDING ALBUM

My mother showed us her wedding picture from 1948. She wanted us to see her white gown. She was thin and had a long nose then. Ruby wore a ruffled tuxedo shirt. His face was poked out.

My mother had punched Ruby's face out of all the photographs. Here he is faceless with his arm around my grandmother's shoulder. Here he is faceless dancing with my aunt.

TO MOTOR CITY

Maury Cohen gave Ruby a job as a buyer in Detroit.

Ruby told Lenie that he couldn't visit her when she was sick because he had followed Pat to Detroit. He wanted to marry her. Pat refused.

Ruby told Beverly that Pat followed him to Detroit because she wanted to marry him. Ruby promised. He stalled.

NEW PAD ON WEST FOSTER

Maury transferred Ruby back to Chicago. Pat returned too.

Ruby told Lenie that he proposed to Pat. She turned him down again.

Ruby told Beverly that Pat pleaded to marry him. He put her off.

Ruby said that he didn't want to marry Pat. He had someone else in mind.

WHAT TO DO WITH US

Ruby picked us up every other Saturday. He never knew what to do with us. Sometimes he took us to the movies and fell asleep.

Ruby's bachelor apartment was not set up for children. When we complained about being bored, he told us to go play on the highway. We said it was too far away, so he offered to drive us.

When he didn't feel like driving us, Ruby told us to bang our heads against the wall. Then he changed his mind. "Come to think of it," he said, "you might hurt the wall."

When Ruby said that he was not going to let inmates run the asylum, it meant that the asylum was not happy with the inmates.

IMPORTANT LESSONS

At Manny's Cafeteria and Delicatessen in the South Loop, Ruby taught us that a bagel is a delivery system for cream cheese.

The only seeds of value are poppy seeds.

Mohnstrudel can change your life, but don't call it poppy-seed strudel. That shows you don't know what you're talking about.

Cottage cheese seems bland, but it is a binge food.

You betcha, fried salami scrambled eggs are the best breakfast.

Don't bother with soft salami. Hard salami is the only salami that matters.

What's existence without a three-pound hard salami hanging in the pantry?

Don't waste space in your drink. Get ice on the side.

Meatloaf with scrambled egg in the middle is a secret weapon.

It ought to be illegal to serve tuna fish without pickled relish.

What's the point of kugel without raisins?

Cheesecake can be good or bad, but there is no such thing as bad rice pudding.

It's a tossup between Jewish spaghetti and spaghetti carbonara, but you don't have to announce it.

Don't embarrass yourself and order white bread on a sandwich.

If someone orders white bread, you know their family came over on the *Mayflower*.

Don't worry about pork in egg rolls, but pork chops are not allowed.

You can stretch the rules for bacon if it's crispy.

If you tip a buck to the guy behind the counter, he'll give you extra-lean meat on your corned beef sandwich. But pastrami is better than corned beef and you don't want that too lean.

Don't get suckered into a thin cut of baloney.

A new pickle is better than an old pickle, but an old pickle is pretty good.

If you want a vegetable, eat a tomato with pickles.

Phooey on Nathan's. The knuckleheads give you a skinny hot dog on a cold bun.

What good is a hot dog if it's not a jumbo on a steamed poppy-seed bun?

Cole slaw, take it or leave it, but piccalilli matters to the bun big-time.

Deli mustard only. Ketchup on a hot dog makes you retch.
Hamburger over steak.

A thick baloney steak is better than filet mignon.

The greatest steak in the world cannot compare to a kosher hot dog.

7

PLAYING THE ODDS

Our father is blowing on dice in the kitchen. He's cupping them in his palms and warming them up for the next play. We're kneeling on the floor, facing the corner, getting ready for the toss. "Bet the seven coming out," he says. "Then we'll see what happens."

THEORY OF BLACKJACK

We are eating soft-serve ice-cream cones in the car home. "The dealer is showing a six," Ruby says. "You have sixteen. What's your play?"

GENETIC CARDS

We were playing War. "You're all mixed up," Ruby said. "You have your mother's face, but my hands."

AMBIVALENCE

Ruby said that his mother adored him. He also said that he made her ill. She died because of him.

A WIFE FOR ALL SEASONS

Ruby had different wives. We couldn't always recall their names. They were of the working variety. They were seasonal, like weather.

SINGING GONDOLIERS

Ruby wooed his dates at the Villa Venice on Milwaukee Avenue in Wheeling. You could ride in a gondola on the Des Plaines River. Singing gondoliers serenaded you through the canals. Long limousines ferried you from the supper club to the Quonset Hut, a casino where you rubbed shoulders with the smart set and lost money to the Mob.

IN THE GRANDSTANDS

Ruby took us to our first Cubs game. He taught us how to keep score. Lenie loved it. We could get anything we wanted from the vendors. One dropped a five-dollar bill. Lenie pocketed it. Ruby was impressed. We were grandstanders.

HEDGING

Ruby rooted for the home team and bet on the visitors. That way he won either way. He also lost.

BOOKIE

Ruby explained that a bookmaker is not someone who makes books. It's someone who fixes them.

STEAM

Ruby and Jookie took me to the Russian schvitz. We peered through the steam. It was like fog on a window. We poured buckets of ice water over our heads. Men in long towels moved around like ghosts. They made English sound like a foreign language. In the restaurant, I drank strawberry pop. I wondered why my face was red when I looked in the mirror.

HAROLD THE TURTLE

We were not allowed to have pets. Ruby gave us five turtles. The largest sat on all the others until he suffocated the whole family. We called him *Harold*.

ON CRITICISM

Whenever you made fun of yourself, Ruby quickly agreed. But if you grumbled about something, he took a different tack. "Don't expect me to listen to that," he said. "If you've got a complaint, take it to City Hall."

CAMP DAKOMA

Jookie was part owner of Camp Dakoma. He lost money to Ruby in a gin game. They cooked up a deal for us to go to camp one summer for free. A yellow school bus picked us up. Lenie liked making lanyards, but I hated everything. This was a regular day camp. You've got to be kidding me—we're irregulars!

AT AUNT ELAINE AND UNCLE BOB'S

Ruby took us to his sister's house to hang out with our cousins Jeff and Earl. Jeff was older, Earl our age. We could play with electric trains in the basement. We could hit baseballs in the empty lot next door. It was a good place to park for a meal, too. Uncle Bob grilled in the backyard. Aunt Elaine grilled us about our mom. She complained about losing touch. We told our mom about it. She harrumphed.

THE COLLECTION BUSINESS

Uncle Bob was in the collection business. He had phone numbers
written down on little strips of paper. Upstairs we could hear him
threatening people on the line.

UNCLE BOB IN THE GALLERY

"You skipped your payments."

   "Don't be a deadbeat."

   "You're embarrassing yourself."

   "I've heard that one before."

   "The bank doesn't care about your problems."

   "You should have thought of that when you bought it."

   "Every sucker has a story."

   "I'd leave too if I were her."

   "I feel sorry for your children."

   "We know where you live."

THE TIGER FAMILY

Aunt Elaine wore heels and worked in a dress shop. She was coiffed. Others could look around. She preferred her own kingdom of men. She loved her husband, Bob. They held hands in bed at night. She was devoted to her younger son, Earl. He was her superpower. Most of all, she adored her elder son, Jeffrey. She considered him the most handsome male on the planet. She would have been his prom queen if she could. She would have married him. Poor Bob. Oedipus Jeffrey would have been king.

LOYALTY OATH

Elaine was cool with her younger brother, Prince Harold. Whatever he did was fine with her. The only time she ever talked back to him was when he ticked off Jeff—that was not okay. Otherwise, he could have murdered someone in the street and she wouldn't make a peep.

SPEAKING OF MURDER

Aunt Elaine complained that Uncle Bob let the kids "get away with murder." Ruby looked at her wistfully. "If only."

———

MARKUP

Ruby taught us a business game called *Markup*. You had to guess the price spread between what something cost to produce and what it sold for. We asked if our mom knew how to play too. "Yes," he said, "she's excellent." It was the only time we ever heard him say anything positive about her.

A PENNY FOUND

Ruby flew into a rage if you didn't pick up a penny from the ground. Moolah matters. You can't live on love.

MAKE THEM WORRY

Scrap was a cash business. You were up or down. Everyone was dealing in percentages. Everyone owed everyone else money. It was an honor economy. But there was no dishonor in making people wait to get their dough. "Keep the long green in your own pocket," Ruby told us. "Sometimes people worry when you don't pay them. Worried people negotiate."

HEADS UP

Anyone who says "I'm not the sort of person who tries to cheat you in business" is exactly the sort of person who tries to cheat you in business.

RUBY'S RIDDLE

Q: What's a cosigner?
A: A schmuck with a pen.

WHAT WE OWE NEW YORK

There's no need to thank New York City for inventing credit cards, Ruby taught us, because interest rates can kick your butt.

But you can thank New York City when you wipe your ass because that's where toilet paper was invented.

CHARACTER

Ruby said that he was a good judge of character. He didn't care if the characters were good.

PAY CASH

Ruby carried a huge wad in a money clip. He kept small bills on the outside, like us.

CO-OWNERS

Ruby didn't pay the twenty-five-dollars-a-month child support the court ordered. Instead, he offered a onetime payout. He settled the divorce with half a building on Carroll Avenue. Elaine owned the other half. Irma accepted because she didn't want to chase him down every month for the money.

We never saw this building, because it was located on a subterranean street in an industrial neighborhood on the Near West Side. It was hard to get to on foot. Railroad tracks ran down the center of the avenue. No one wanted to rent this property on an old freight corridor lined by loading docks. It was a place for scrap.

Ruby complained that he never received credit for the gift.

Irma and Elaine stopped speaking to each other when they sold the property.

My mom thought she was cheated on the sale. Ruby said, "You know my sister and you know your mom. Now who do you think got the better of who?"

MAN TO MAN

Ruby sat me down on his living-room couch. He wanted to have a heart-to-heart. "Your mother is frigid," he said. "The only real woman is a prostitute."

WOMAN TO WOMAN

My mother leaned forward on Lenie's bed. She had something significant to tell her about marriage: "A woman has to be a whore in bed for her husband."

INNUENDO

Someone is a prude. Someone else is a prick. Prudes hate pricks. Pricks don't stand for prudes.

ROLE MODELS

My mom admired women who were elegant, sexy, mysterious, and untouchable while my father's perfect women were prostitutes who worked for free.

UNFILTERED

Ruby and Irma both smoked. They thought filters were for cigarettes.

JUST A SUGGESTION

Wait until your children are teenagers before trashing the sexual proclivities of your ex-wife and ex-husband.

8

PORTRAIT OF MY GRANDFATHER

Like Isaac Babel, the Russian writer from Odesa, my grandfather was "a man with spectacles on his nose and autumn in his heart."

HOMEGROWN THEOLOGY

We were standing in the market. "Do you know the difference between this can of tomatoes and God?" my grandfather asked.

"God is fresh and not canned?" I ventured.

"No. God does not have an expiration date."

MY FIRST BOOKSTORE

My grandfather liked to hang around Moishe Cheshinsky's bookstore on Lawrence Avenue. We were usually the only ones in the stacks.

The back room was dusty. Most of the books were written in languages I couldn't understand. I wondered, "Why do you like it here so much?"

My grandfather gestured toward the shelves, "This is my other family."

THE MASSES

My grandfather believed we were People of the Book. His friend Meyer believed in the Book of the People.

Meyer was a mensch who wanted to improve the world,

Grandpa explained, but he was going about it all wrong. That's because he was still a Communist. He had missed the news bulletin about Stalin.

Meyer said, "The masses are no asses."

My grandfather shook his head. "Are you certain about that?"

Meyer's slogan "Private property is theft" was not put to the test because no one wanted to steal books from Cheshinsky's store. There was never much to take in the till.

POOR YHWH

My grandfather's friend said he felt sorry for the Holy One, blessed be His name, which you should not pronounce, because YHWH had so many problems with evil that He had to withdraw from the world.

GENESIS 1 AND 2

The old men seemed ancient to me—they were in their early sixties—and should have had beards. They didn't like the organized part of religion, but they loved the Hebrew Bible.

My grandpa's cronies debated everything. They had no interest in sports—this was their favorite pastime.

One day they argued about the origin of the world. Everyone had a theory about why Yahweh created mankind twice.

There was a newcomer in the corner. "So what?" he said finally. "The second time was no better than the first."

ASHKENAZIM

The old men spoke with accents. They had fled pogroms, or ten years of military service, or bad marriages. They checked *Other* on government forms because they did not consider themselves *White*. That was for gentiles. "Use your keppie," my grandfather said, which meant my noggin. "We're not white. We're Jewish."

OY

My grandfather resorted to Yiddish when he was frustrated. He said *oy Gutt* (oh my God) or *oy gevalt* (good grief). But I got confused and mixed up God and grief.

ARISTOTLE ON LAWRENCE AVENUE

"I do believe the Messiah will come, but he is taking a long time to get here." It took me thirty years to discover my grandfather was paraphrasing Maimonides in *The Guide for the Perplexed*.

HOW MY GRANDPARENTS MET

Anna was selling newspapers in a kiosk on Orchard Street on the Lower East Side of New York. Oscar was buying.

GETTING TO THE ALTAR

Anna liked it that Oscar liked books. It went over well with her mother. Personally, she did not care to read. She preferred cards.

Oscar was an Eastern European, who had classical tastes. Anna was an American, who did not.

Anna was proud of the fact that she was born in New York City. It was more of an accomplishment than being born in Riga, like her husband.

Oscar was quiet, but he had fervent opinions. Sometimes he stood on a soapbox and started shouting in Union Square. Anna was mortified.

I asked my grandmother what my grandfather was so passionate about. She said, "It had something to do with politics."

I tried to nail it down and asked what countries were involved. "I think it was Spain," she said. "Or maybe it was Portugal."

Anna did not have suitors. Oscar seemed suitable. He wore a coat and tie. Anna was the love of his life.

Anna was practical, Oscar was not. It was time for the practical and the impractical one to get married. They weren't getting any younger. They needed to get going on a family. She did what she needed to. There was only one way.

HONEYMOON PHOTO

I have a photograph of my grandfather standing in front of railroad tracks with two heavy suitcases. His hat is pushed back on his balding head. He looks happy to be going wherever he is going with my grandmother, who is missing from the picture.

OLD TIME RELIGION

My grandfather followed his younger sister to Rochester, New York. He went into the kosher meat business. But he went broke because he refused to pay off a group of crooked rabbis. They wouldn't certify his meat. After that, he never entered a synagogue, though sometimes he stood outside and listened to the prayers.

DER TOG

My grandfather got a job traveling through the Midwest selling ads for the Yiddish daily *Der Tog* (The Day). He didn't drive and took trains everywhere. I asked my grandmother what it was like for him navigating states like Illinois, Iowa, and Nebraska. "There were very few takers," she said. "It was meshuga."

KEEPING COMPANY

After my grandfather transferred to the Midwest, he took a room in a boardinghouse on the North Side of Chicago. My grandmother was still living in Rochester with their two daughters. Someone saw him taking a walk with the widow Schulman in West Rogers Park. It was rumored that they were keeping company. The next week my grandmother packed up and moved to Chicago.

THE SIDEWALKS IN CHICAGO

Irma and Bea remembered walking from the train station in downtown Chicago. Their mother was carrying two suitcases and tripped and fell. She exclaimed, "Even the sidewalks in Chicago are crooked!"

BAD SIGNS

My grandparents wanted to rent in Logan Square. There were signs on apartment buildings that said, "No dogs or Jews allowed." Hatred is no joke. They moved to another block.

IN THE OLD COUNTRY

There were signs on apartment buildings that said, "No Jews or Devils Welcome." In the New Country, dogs were disruptive, but devils were not a problem.

A SECRET SOAPBOXER

The family settled down. My grandfather seemed calm, but every now and then he got back up on a soapbox and started shouting about politics in Bughouse Square. He was so soft-spoken that I could never square it. Neither could anyone else in the family. My grandmother said he sounded like a lunatic.

SOAPBOX PREACHERS

The Moody Bible Institute was close to Bughouse Square. According to my grandmother, the only difference was that their crackpots quoted scripture.

ENCYCLOPEDIC

After his heart attack, my grandfather was dropped by *The Day*. He couldn't get picked up by *The Forward* either. The Yiddish newspapers didn't need a traveling salesman who couldn't travel.

Every day my grandfather walked door to door trying to sell *The Book of Knowledge* to people who couldn't afford it. He was knowledgeable, but they knew enough not to buy.

EXILE ON MAXWELL STREET

My grandpa had to put down his books and start selling discount clothes on Maxwell Street. He discounted the experience. He was back to peddling schmattes. My poor grandfather—he hated working in what was called "the poor Jew quarter." He wouldn't let us visit him.

HISTORY LESSON

Chicago was incorporated in 1833. The first Jews were street peddlers. Their first religious service was the Day of Atonement.

CHICAGO BLUES

The Maxwell Street Market was filled with hucksters, hawkers, and blues musicians, who plugged their instruments into the storefronts. They needed to outshout the radios. One night when he was closing up my grandfather heard Howlin' Wolf sing "Crying at Daybreak."

BITTER MEMORY

My mother hated the fact that my grandmother left the house to play cards at night. She put a covered dish in the refrigerator for my grandfather to heat up after he got home from work.

THE ARGUMENT

My grandmother argued with my grandfather. He refused to argue with her. He did not believe in raising your voice. Whenever she started yelling at him, he went to the front hall closet and put on his hat, coat, and muffler. Without saying a word, he left the house.

FIRST DOLL

Bea was throwing a tantrum. Her dad said, "Dolly, cut it out." But Bea did not cut it out. Instead, she threw an even greater tantrum. He got so exasperated that he slapped her. This was the only time he ever hit anyone. He recoiled and rushed out of the house. He came home with a gift. This was Dolly's first doll.

THE SILENT TREATMENT

My grandmother often punished her daughters with "the silent treatment." She didn't speak to them for days at a time. Bea said that she spent half her life not hearing her mother's voice.

Once my grandmother took Bea for a dress fitting when she

was still not talking to her. She spoke to the clerk instead: "Tell the drunk it's still too long."

INFLUENZA

My grandmother didn't talk about her early life. She didn't tell us that she got the flu in the epidemic of 1918. We found out from Auntie Bea that she transmitted it to her father, Isaac, and her younger sister, Sarah, who both died.

ON NOT BECOMING A DENTIST

My mother said, "Your grandfather should have become a dentist." She told me so many times it made my teeth hurt.

A LATVIAN JEW IN AMERICA

When he got to New York as a teenager, my grandfather did not go to school. He went to work. He was smart, but he did not have a head for business. "It was a misfortune," my mother said. "He never figured out how to be an American in America."

COMMUNIST IN A KIOSK

We found out from my mom that my grandfather had a brother named Zalman, who lived in Leningrad, which my grandfather called St. Petersburg. They were not in touch. All she knew was that her uncle was a Communist who worked in a kiosk. "Except he's not really a Communist," she said, "and there's nothing to sell."

VACATION IN MIAMI BEACH

It was eighty degrees. We were wearing bathing suits. On the beach, my grandfather wore a hat with flaps and a long winter coat. He shook sand from his dress shoes.

THE BABYSITTER

My grandmother played poker on Saturday night. My grandfather babysat us. We were noisy. He was noiseless. When Lenie and I fought, he threatened to leave. That always calmed us down.

Grandpa copied poems into the backs of his books. He whispered to himself. When he was writing, my grandfather entered another world. I wondered where he had gone and wanted to go there too.

Lenie and I never asked our grandfather to read to us. Instead, we just romped through the house. Eventually, we settled next to him on the couch and fell asleep in his lap.

POET UNKNOWN

It wasn't until I started writing poetry in high school that I asked about my grandfather's poems. I wondered if they were written in Hebrew, Yiddish, or English. No one knew.

My mother waved away the question—the fact that he wrote poetry only proved that he couldn't adapt to the New World.

My aunt thought that maybe his poems were political, and she wasn't interested in politics.

My grandmother said that it was pointless to make notes in books that were published. The books were hard to understand. After he died, she gave them away to a Jewish charity.

My grandmother, my aunt, and my mother could see I was upset about my grandfather's library. They might have come up with a cover story. It's possible my grandmother just tossed the books into the trash.

INAUGURATION DAY, 1957

I realized the country celebrated my birthday every four years. This year it was a day late. It didn't invite us to its party.

My grandfather was sorry Eisenhower was reelected president.

Not liking Ike was a Democratic tradition. Grandpa said, "He's better at playing golf than running a country."

COTTON CANDY

My grandfather and I walked on the bridge over the Chicago River. It was our last walk together. I held his hand and ate cotton candy—that sugary air, that sweet blue light spun out of nothing.

NO CHILDREN ON THE FIFTH FLOOR

Our grandfather had another heart attack. They wouldn't let Lenie and me in the hospital to visit. We stood on the hood of a car in the parking lot across the street. We could see him in the window on the fifth floor. He was tall and distant in his hospital gown. We waved to him wildly. He kissed his fingers and pressed them to the glass.

IN MEMORY OF OSCAR GINSBURG

The first death. The first time you pick up a shovel and toss dirt onto the coffin. The first time you hear that thud. The first time you say Kaddish. The first time you place a stone by a grave. The first time you make a vow.

————

A PLOT

My grandfather was buried in Westlawn Cemetery in Norridge. There was an empty plot for my grandmother next to him.

A NEW HAT

For fifty years, my mother regretted that her father passed away before he could wear the new gray hat he bought for Passover.

THE JAYWALKER

You would not have pegged him as a jaywalker, but after his death my mother found twelve tickets in his bottom drawer.

SAVIOR LIST

Lenie scoured her memory. She wondered if she had accidentally left our grandfather's name out of her bedtime prayers. His death might be her fault.

SPELLBOUND 1

After the funeral, I wandered down to the basement and picked an anthology off the shelf. I found a poem called "Spellbound." I fell under its spell. The author's name was not included. I decided my grandfather must have written it. There was something he was trying to tell me.

SPELLBOUND 2

When I was in high school, I found the same poem in an anthology of English poetry. It was written by Emily Brontë. I was spellbound all over again, but I was also confused. Who was trying to reach me?

SPELLBOUND 3

I used to lie on my bed at night and imagine my grandfather's missing poems. I put myself into a spell. Then I wrote what I imagined.

DARK NIGHT

My grandfather taught me to leave a crack in the shutters so you can tell when it is morning.

9

ALBANY PARK

After my grandfather died, my grandmother moved to a small studio apartment in a large building in Albany Park. The neighborhood on the northwest side was named after Albany, New York. That's where the streetcar magnate DeLancy Louderback was born. Too bad he didn't come from Rochester.

My grandmother lived on Bernard and Lawrence in a Jewish neighborhood with dress shops, synagogues, and Chinese restaurants.

Jews were already moving out of the declining neighborhood when my grandmother moved in, which is why she could afford it.

My grandfather never wanted my grandmother to work. He would have been appalled that she got a job in the coat department at Three Sisters on State and Monroe. She commuted on the Ravenswood "L" from Lawrence and Kimball to the heart of downtown Chicago.

She liked making her own money. I once asked her if she had any regrets in life. She said, "I should have gotten a job earlier."

ON BEING ALONE

My grandmother never said she was lonely. But she turned on the television set as soon as she got home from work. The voices soothed her while she cooked.

GREEN COUCH

My grandmother was proud of her electric-green couch. There was a time when that color was in fashion. Or maybe there was just a place.

The couch, which was big and heavy, was covered in a thick plastic seat cover. Grandma unzipped it for company, but she almost never had company. Family didn't count.

One day I would inherit my grandmother's green couch in near-perfect condition. I kept it in my study and moved it from city to city for thirty years. All my difficult reading took place on that couch, which was comfortable for naps. Everyone commented on the color. No one liked it but me.

THE SEAMSTRESS

Our grandmother's friend Garber had an apartment right across the hall on the second floor. They huffed up a winding set of stairs together. Grandma called her by her last name, like a man.

I tagged along when my sisters got their clothes hemmed. Garber sat on the floor with straight pins in her mouth, shortening pants or skirts. She was a legendary gossip who talked out of both sides of her mouth.

PORTRAIT OF MARY MURIN

Mary Murin was my grandmother's best friend. We called her Mary, Grandma called her Murin. They lived nearby. They played cards together.

Murin had a guy. He was a basic Joe. He drove them to games for gas money.

Murin had two Dobermans named Lucky. When Lucky #1 died, she got another Doberman. He was named Lucky Jr. All her dogs were scary and Lucky.

Murin had the phlegmy voice of a smoker. She was scary, but not fortunate. She had a daughter named *Davita*. The name means Beloved, but they were estranged.

Murin was a bruiser. She blew her nose in cloth napkins. She wore her hose rolled down around her ankles. I asked her why she didn't roll them up to her knees. She said, "Circulation."

My grandmother and Murin came out fighting. They didn't need a bell. Every day they talked. Every day they fought. It was not a lover's quarrel. It was a lover's brawl.

Murin and my grandmother always made up. The fight needed to end each night so it could start again each morning.

A MOMENT OF MUSIC

My grandmother's friend Ida Silvertrust had a heavy Hungarian accent. She was the only person I knew who could play classical piano. I liked to observe her hands. Her specialty was Liszt's nineteen Hungarian Rhapsodies.

Ida piled her hair on top of her head. She was a widow, like my grandmother. I liked her name because she was someone I trusted.

Ida reminisced while she played. Her husband had been killed in a robbery in front of their store. Whenever she talked about him, she started weeping and switched to nocturnes.

IN THE METRO

My grandmother once took us to the Metro Theatre. The screen was behind you when you entered and so you swiveled around and watched the movie backwards. People who arrived late looked like they were entering the film.

KRADER'S LIVE POULTRY STORE

Q: Who wants to stand in chicken feathers and watch Mr. Krader kill one live chicken after the next?

A: The same women who stand in long lines in the St. Louis Fish Market and watch Mr. Cutler grind suckers for gefilte fish.

CHESHINSKY'S BOOKSTORE

My grandmother preferred my grandfather's hangout when it was on Division Street. It was easier to avoid. But she still managed.

THREE OF US

My grandmother liked to take Lenie and me downtown. On Saturdays we met her at work so that she could buy us a late lunch at Fritzel's. She could not afford it. The three of us sat in a red leather booth with white tablecloths. There were crystal glasses on the table. We eyed celebrities. We were swells!

We waited for grandma to get off work. Then we went to the movies. Unlike our parents, our grandmother sprang for chocolate raisins and nonpareils. She was the sportiest one in the family.

My grandmother kept us in the Loop. Sometimes she took us to Ronny's Original Steak House for dinner. It was a palace where you could get a steak, salad, and baked potato for $1.19.

My grandmother took us to feed the pigeons in front of the Chicago Civic Center. We couldn't compete with the pigeon man. He had birds all over his arms and shoulders. But there were always a few smart pigeons who wandered over for stale challah.

OFF TO ROCHESTER

My grandmother spent her vacations in Rochester. She went to the kosher butcher with her sister-in-law. They stopped in the bar across the street to split a beer. There was nothing wrong with getting a little tipsy in the afternoon.

Unlike her husband, my grandmother did not spit when she passed a rabbi on the street. But she didn't go into the synagogue either.

My grandmother took us with her for our holidays. Why go skiing in the Alps? There's plenty of snow in Rochester. Why summer in Saint-Tropez? There's plenty of sun in Rochester.

ROCHESTER RELATIVES

My aunt and uncle Celia and Max Deutsch grew up together in a shtetl in Russia. They were first cousins, who married and migrated to New York.

Max decided that New York City was for peddlers. Opportunity was in Rochester.

Max and Celia had three children, my older cousins Sherwood, Larry, and Roselyn.

My grandmother could not get over Max's extravagance. He had twenty pairs of shoes. "Let's hop in the car," he said to her, "and go buy crystal in Canada." She came home with six crystal glass decanters, twenty-four crystal glasses, and a bottle of cognac.

AUNT CELIA AT THE STOVE

I glimpsed my grandfather's profile on his younger sister's face.

COUSIN SHERWOOD

Sherwood drove through his hometown like a race car driver with an engine on fire. We sat plastered to the backseat. He wasn't drunk. We were hurrying to his store.

Sherwood started out as a pharmacist in a small pharmacy. Then he bought the bigger pharmacy. Then he bought the liquor store next to the big pharmacy. Then he stopped prescribing drugs and started recommending wines.

Sherwood learned about grapes and vineyards. The wine craze built him the largest liquor store in New York State. It was called Century Liquors. It almost took that long to walk through it.

My grandmother wheeled a shopping cart down the aisles. Sherwood begged her to fill it up. He was just like his father—she could have anything she wanted. But my grandmother wasn't a drinker. She could never think of anything to take.

COUSIN LARRY

Larry was a phantom. We never saw him. He had "nerves." My grandmother didn't believe in the diagnosis. She wanted Larry to live with her. Voices were raised. She was outvoted. Larry lived in a facility somewhere. We were not there when he visited home, but we heard that the kitchen knives were hidden.

COUSIN ROSELYN

Rossie came to visit. She was the family beauty. She spent a lot of time in front of a vanity getting ready for dates. I never thought anyone stacked up. In the Deutsch family, it was rumored that you could marry your cousin. I was ready to propose. But I was too young to date her.

F.A.P.

Your parents are whispering about F.A.P. This is something ominous that strikes people in Rochester.

Everyone in the family seems to have it. You don't know what it is. It has something to do with polyps in the colon, whatever those are, wherever that is.

F.A.P. seems to cause cancer. And cancer is like polio. You don't want to catch it.

10

IT'S 1958

Swivel your hips! It's the year of Wham-O. I was too young for the bunny hop, right on time for the hula hoop.

PARALLEL PLAY

Irma was rocking a new cradle while Ruby was rocking a new nightclub.

WHAT A DOG!

Ruby bumped into Beverly at an after-hours club. He offered to lend her his car if she gave him a lift home. She loved the way he played with Doodles, a black cocker spaniel. He was a nurturer! She decided he would make a fantastic father.

WHAT A LOSER!

Beverly Cohen lived on Beverly Green Drive in Beverly Woods. She worked in Beverly Hills. She was living the full Beverly life as a legal secretary. When she flew back to California, her boyfriend met her at the airport. He was wearing droopy drawer shorts, slop sandals, baggy sweat socks. The Beverly dream had a deadbeat in it. When the deadbeat dropped her off, she dropped him.

MARRIAGE PROPOSAL

Beverly wrote a long letter proposing to Ruby. He was the love of her life. She couldn't decide whether to send it. Women didn't propose to men. It wasn't done.

Then Aunt Sally called. Aunt Sally was a former model. She was avant-garde in the divorce department. She had two under her belt. It was no big deal.

Aunt Sally said, "Send it for God's sake. You're twenty-seven years old. A bad marriage is better than no marriage. You can't keep sleeping around without being divorced. There's a stigma to it."

THE PHONE CALL

Beverly sent the letter. Ruby called right away. He asked her if she was preggers. That would have made it easy to say yes.

Beverly wasn't pregnant. She wanted to marry for love.

Ruby was a stand-up guy, but he had learned his lesson. Marriage was lunacy. He said, "Then why bother with the whole mishigas?"

Ruby was in bad shape. He said he wasn't fit for a family.

NOW OR NEVER

Beverly told her brother, Jordan, what had happened. He said, "What's wrong with you? That's no way to propose. You've got to do it in person." He sent her a plane ticket.

Ruby showed the letter to Maury, his card partner and boss. Maury said, "You're running around like a madman. You've got a chance to be respectable. Take it."

The name *Cohen* means "priest." Maury Cohen was an unlikely one.

Ruby met Beverly at the airport. He accepted at the gate. Beverly's mother was no longer alive. She would have been ecstatic. They told her father and his new wife, Fritzi. Tevele was skeptical—he wanted a scholar. Fritzi was pleased—she wanted a party.

Fritzi opened a calendar to set a date. Harold closed it and said, "We're not waiting. It's now or never."

Three weeks later was now.

THE LETTER

Ruby always said it was the letter. Whenever he hit a low point, he pulled it out and read it. Then he put it away again. He kept it for the rest of his life.

THE BIG DAY

Ruby and Beverly were married under the chuppah at Fritzi's house in West Rogers Park. Everyone in their families was there except us. Lenie and I didn't know we were invited. My mom declined for us.

DURING THE HONEYMOON

Pat had keys to the apartment on West Foster Avenue. While Ruby and Beverly celebrated their honeymoon in Los Angeles, Pat stole Doodles. Bucky had a new dog! The nurturer had lost his pet. Ruby didn't watch out for Pat, so Pat took the new television set too.

HAROLD'S CLUB

The newlyweds drove Beverly's 1953 black-and-white Chevy Bel Air sedan back to Chicago. They went via Hearst Castle, San Francisco, and then east to Lake Tahoe. Ruby wanted to avoid Las Vegas. He was playing it straight. They ended up in Reno, which didn't count because it was rinky-dink: nickel blackjack, ten-cent craps. You couldn't fall too far off the wagon. When Ruby and Beverly pulled into the downtown strip, they saw enormous block letters in neon lights: HAROLD'S CLUB. Harold was Ruby's given name. It was the sign.

WEDDING MONEY

Ruby cased the joint for Beverly. He was like a tour guide from the Vatican checking out a small church.

They sidled up to a craps table. The minimum bet was twenty-five cents. Ruby gave five hundred dollars to the stick man to convert to chips. It was like blowing a whistle. Everything halted.

The pit bosses came running over. Ruby put twenty-five dollars on the pass line. He put three bucks on the high-low eleven. He hit the eleven. He let it ride. He hit the seven. Beverly brought him luck. He kept hitting the numbers. They walked away with eleven hundred dollars. That would be eleven thousand today.

Two hosts descended. They fell all over themselves. Ruby and Beverly got the honeymoon suite. They were comped for everything.

The newlyweds checked out the next morning. They never went back to Reno—it was too sweet.

A LONG MARRIAGE

You could describe it as a marriage that lasted for forty-six years and yielded two children, seven grandchildren, and eight great-grandchildren. You could also say Beverly left Beverly Hills so Harold could take her to a casino.

––––––

A CANTOR GOES SMELTING

Beverly's father bankrolled them to a small lead-smelting dealership and scrap operation. Junk was performing well. Ruby was back in business, davening for copper in Chicago.

TWO FATHERS, ONE ROOM

Ruby sat in the living room chatting with Kurt. The days of Daddy Ruby and Daddy Kurt were gone. Lenie and I were careful not to call anyone anything.

WHAT'S THE DIFFERENCE?

Kurt played in a weekly gin game for a twentieth of a cent a point. Ruby played in a weekly gin game for a dollar a point. Kurt rummaged around for a pack of cards. Ruby carried one in his jacket. Kurt was studiously fair. Ruby was the opposite. "I don't care how I win," he said. "I want the upper hand."

THE BLACK SOX

Everyone knew the White Sox threw the World Series in 1919. Kurt blamed the scandal on the kingpin Arnold Rothstein, who was nicknamed *The Fixer*. Ruby called it differently. "You've got to admire *The Big Bankroll*," he said. "They never convicted him of nothing, but he pocketed $350,000."

AIR RAID

We thought the Soviets were bombing us when the air-raid sirens blared at 10:30 p.m. My parents made us hide under our beds. But we were not at war. Something else hysterical had happened. The Go-Go Sox clinched the pennant.

THE SMOKERS

Kurt smoked Winstons. He quit out of cheapness. But he bummed singles whenever he could. The rest of the time he substituted with Dentyne gum.

Irma's package of Luckies lasted over a year. She had a cigarette holder, but she didn't smoke. She liked to dangle it from her hand by the swimming pool.

Ruby smoked unfiltered Viceroys. Then he switched to menthol Kools. It was easier on his throat. He needed his voice to shout normally.

SNUFFERS

Irma wanted to snuff out candles with a long silver-handled candle snuffer. Ruby wanted to snuff out enemies with a snub-nosed pistol. She owned the snuffer. He never touched a pistol. Neither did she. No one was snuffing anyone.

THE UNTOUCHABLES

No one touched the television set when you were watching *The Untouchables* at 9:30 on Thursday night. Kurt thought it was criminal when the last season moved to Tuesday. He played cards then. But we didn't see a problem. His gin game was legal. His pals could drink moonshine in the open.

GENTLEMAN'S AGREEMENT

Irma and Kurt liked the movie *Gentleman's Agreement* with Gregory Peck as an undercover Jewish journalist who exposes anti-Semitism in New York and Connecticut. But we didn't need an actor to tell us the score. We had our own northern suburbs on the lake.

BUTTERFIELD 8

My mother sneaked us into a matinee of *BUtterfield 8*. She loved Elizabeth Taylor as a promiscuous socialite named Gloria Wandrous, who scrawls *No Sale* in lipstick on the mirror. My mother was not promiscuous. But she wanted that mink coat.

My mom loved the movie so much that she read the novel. In real life, Gloria Wandrous was the beautiful tragedy named Starr Faithfull. John O'Hara was Shakespeare.

MURDER, INC.

Ruby took us to see an early showing of *Murder, Inc.* It's about two killers from Brownsville. We had to look away when one of them whips an icepick from his pocket and punches holes in someone's ribs. Ruby closed his eyes too. "I always wanted to be a gangster," he confided. "I just didn't have the guts."

WHITE HEAT

Ruby's favorite movie was the gangster classic *White Heat*. My mom was nonplussed when I came home quoting James Cagney: "Made it, Ma! Top of the world!"

She knew where I was coming from. "Leave it to Ruby," she said, "and you'll get blown off a gas tank."

HORSE SENSE

Ruby also loved Jimmy Cagney as a murderous thug in *The Public Enemy*—that was his #2.

The horse scene was based on a true story. Ruby liked Two Gun Alterie and his guys for executing the horse that trampled Nails Morton to death in Lincoln Park. He was always up for retaliation.

Lenie and me? We sided with the horse.

JEWISH GANGSTERS

Ruby had a soft spot for the Purple Gang from the East Side of Detroit. It was as if he knew the four Burnstein brothers who grew up together in "Little Jerusalem." They were small-time thugs who hit it big smuggling whiskey from Canada to Chicago during Prohibition.

The Purples were famous in our part of town because the North Side Gang hijacked their booze and got whacked in the St. Valentine's Day Massacre. Ruby lived near North Clark Street, and we drove by the execution site all the time.

Ruby also had fellow feeling for the Cleveland Syndicate, whose bootleg outfit on Lake Erie was called "the Little Jewish Navy." That was a military he could get behind.

But Bugsy Siegel and Meyer Lansky were by far his two favorite gangsters. He would have loved to join the Bugs and Meyer mob, but he was too young and soft. If he had been tougher, he could have founded Las Vegas.

Meyer Lansky was minted Maier Suchowljansky. Bugsy Siegel was born Benjamin Siegelbaum. Belarus or Brooklyn, Ruby's guys knew where they came from, and what they were leaving: poverty.

Gangster Mickey Cohen also made Ruby's pantheon. He set up the sports book and created the race wire for Bugsy's hotel on the Vegas Strip, which Meyer transformed into a profit machine for the Chicago Outfit.

"Those guys were geniuses," Ruby marveled. "They could have done anything."

ROUGH JUSTICE

Ruby said that in the thirties a Jewish judge asked Meyer Lansky to break up German American Bund meetings in New York. He couldn't think of another way to stop the Nazi sympathizers. There was one condition: Lansky's gang couldn't murder anyone.

Meyer was the mob's accountant, but he accepted the challenge. His gang destroyed the meetings. They busted heads and broke limbs but didn't kill anybody. Lansky wouldn't take any dough for the job, either. He identified with his people.

For years, I thought this was another one of Ruby's legendizing stories about his gangster hero, but this one turned out to be historically accurate.

MONIKER

Beverly's pet name for Ruby was *Puni*, shorthand for *shayne punim*, which means "pretty face" in Yiddish. Since *shayne* means "pretty" and *punim* means "face," she was calling him *Face*.

11

CONVERSATION WITH MY MOTHER

My mother was heating a can of chicken soup on the stove. "You really shouldn't make fun of me," I said, "you're my mother."

She barely turned her head. "Don't be so sure, kid."

CLOWN SCHOOL

When I made a joke that my mom didn't think was funny, she said: "What is this, clown school?"

When I made a joke that she thought was sort of funny, she said: "I'd give you a C in clown school."

When I made a joke that she thought was genuinely funny she laughed.

Once my mom gave me a B in clown school. "Thanks, Mom," I said, "I'm learning from the best." She turned around. "I'll change that to an A."

A COMPETITIVE SPORT

In our family, humor was a competitive sport. In competitive sports, people get injuries. It's an unfortunate part of the game.

My dad was left out of the game because his sense of humor was in question. But he didn't seem to know he'd been benched.

The School of Hard Knocks was a houseful of insults.

If you hurt someone's feelings, you could wiggle out of it by saying you were "just kidding." It was embarrassing to be overly sensitive.

If you were joking but meant it, we called it "kidding on the square." My mom was an expert at this method. We were her apprentices.

In the schoolyard you could jump on someone and make them take it back, but at home you took it and sulked.

Exaggerating a story was called "overegging the custard." Sometimes this was harmless; other times it was like overplaying your hand at cards. You didn't want to double down on an outright bluff. You had to pull back or risk losing big.

MY GRANDMOTHER'S BED

We helped our grandmother pull the Murphy bed out of the wall. The bed rocked. We felt as if we were sleeping at sea. Grandma let down her hair. She played a wind instrument in her sleep. In the morning, we pushed the bed back into its hideaway. It was like putting the night away when we closed the wooden doors and the bed disappeared without a trace.

UNDER THE TABLE

You were beating your grandmother at gin rummy.

"I've got you now, Grandma," you crowed.

"Don't get carried away," she said. "Your feet are still under the table."

This was her tell. She had been letting you win. Now she was going to kick your ass.

LET SLEEPING DOGS ROAM FREE

My mother said that our Irish setter, Red, was killed in the street by a car. We sobbed for days. A few years later she let it slip that the dog was living on a farm in northern Wisconsin. She never told us the truth because she didn't want us to be mad at her for giving it away.

LATE FOR SCHOOL

My mother screamed that we were late for school. Our dad rushed us to the car. We raced through the streets. There was no traffic. When we got to Peterson it was locked. We shouted for help and tried the padlocked doors. We peered through the barred windows. No one came to let us in. My dad checked his watch: 5 a.m. My mom had misread the time.

IRMA'S HOME REMEDY

I went for the upset stomach. Lenie went for the headache. Irma's home remedy was crushed aspirin fizzling in warm cola. That will settle an upset stomach. It will soothe a headache. It had better. There's no backup remedy.

WILLPOWER

Some sacrifices are worth making. My mom was violently allergic to fish. But she loved lox so much that she ate it every Sunday morning. For almost a year her hands and lips broke out in a terrible rash. She looked distorted. But over time she built up tolerance and her reaction subsided. Eventually, she didn't show many symptoms at all.

THE TEST

I inherited my allergy to fish from my mother. She was the block. I was the chip. If the block could do it, she reasoned, laying out a fillet of brined salmon, then so could the chip.

"Let's see if he's still allergic," my mother said. I tried to hide but it was too late—my fate was sealed.

The family gathered at the kitchen table. I took a bite of lox and bagel. It tasted salty. I took another bite. Everyone leaned forward to see what would happen.

What happened was that my eyes teared up, a rash broke out

across my lips, and my throat started to swell shut. I had trouble breathing. I backed away from the table gasping.

"Yep," my mother said, "he's still allergic."

THE KISS

When my mom ate lox and kissed me on the cheek, my cheek looked like a piece of lox.

When my mom ate nuts and kissed me on the forehead, my forehead puffed up like a package of nuts.

ON THE FARM

We visited a farm in Wisconsin. I sneezed the entire time. The grass made me sneeze, the hay made me sneeze, and the animals made me sneeze. It is not natural to be allergic to nature.

ON THE FLOOR

I sat on the carpet in the living room because I was allergic to plastic seat covers. Everyone knew the reason, but I liked to pretend that I had come from another culture, somewhere far away, like Japan.

A FEW ALLERGIES FROM CHILDHOOD

Lenie went for quality. She was allergic to penicillin. I went for quantity. I was allergic to fish, nuts, cow's milk, newspaper print, plastic seat covers, dust, pollen, grass, trees, dogs, cats, small creatures of all kinds, and Aunt Idel's voice.

THE ALLERGIST

My mom took me to an allergist. He gave me the arm test. My left arm lit up like a switchboard. I was allergic to everything. The printout went on for ten pages.

My mom rifled through the pages. She was skeptical. "You always overdo it," she said.

The allergist suggested weekly shots. My mom wanted a one-shot solution. We didn't return to the allergist.

RUN, NOSE, RUN

The weather forecast did not call for rain. "Eddie's sneezing," my mom said. "Better bring the umbrella."

I developed an ad hoc system: tissue for school, toilet paper for home, sleeve for car rides, handkerchief for holidays.

My faucet was broken. It leaked all the time.

A FOOT CASE

I was nauseated by dirty socks. It wasn't just other people's socks either. My own made me throw up.

NERVOUS TICS

I didn't know about nervous tics. I would have denied that I had them. But I touched my crotch too often. I scratched my head and sniffed my hand. I jammed a finger into my ear and smelled it. Who knows what else I did to comfort myself?

A BIG HUGGER

My mom was physically affectionate. She was a tremendous hugger. I felt smothered.

ADDENDUM TO FREUD

Freud believed that a man who has been his mother's indisputable favorite always goes through life feeling like a conqueror. I would add that the conqueror has a guilty conscience, a desperate sense of humor, and a host of symptomatic illnesses.

POSTSCRIPT

What sort of conqueror reads Freud?

12

A NEW DEVELOPMENT

There was a new development in Skokie.

My parents bought our house for $20,000. Our address was 5200 Sherwin Avenue.

Our street was named after Ezra R. Sherwin. No one knew who he was, but there was a street named after him in Rogers Park, too.

We were parcel 10-28-314-042. Our lot was 6,200 feet. It was bigger than the others because it was on the corner. Their lots were 4,960 feet.

The color of trim was different. Ours was brown. Otherwise, all the split-level houses looked the same.

We were at a right angle to our neighbors. We faced Sherwin, they fronted Laramie. We were two-way, they were one.

There were twenty houses in our block. I could not tell one from the other. I needed to count whenever I was going to visit someone.

Lenie's friend Robin lived in house 13. Her friend Laura lived in house 14. Everything after that drew a blank.

There were two full blocks in our development: Sherwin and Jarvis. In 1961, the developer squeezed an extra house onto the end of our block. It was too big for its britches and had to face Niles Center Road as a punishment.

That's why there were sixty-one houses in our cluster. Later, someone figured out how to squeeze another half-block onto the grid. It was called Fargo. We never knew anyone who lived over there. You didn't have to go far, but it might as well have been in another county.

Our blocks were rectangular. Frontage Road broke the grid. It curved along the highway. Its purpose was to separate the houses from Edens Expressway. I liked to walk along it. It provided a different avenue of escape from our cul-de-sac.

Every house had a small backyard that bumped up against the alley. The alley was made of gravel. I never went down it until I was seventeen. That's when I worked as a garbageman for the town. The yards were littered with bicycles no one bothered to lock.

Every family had a car. Some families, like ours, quickly moved up to two cars. The average was 1.4.

The cars were made in Detroit. A family with car trouble was a family in trouble. The mechanic was more important than the doctor. You couldn't survive without him.

Every house had a driveway that was eleven feet wide and fourteen feet long. The driveways separated the houses. No one had a garage. There were no fences to make good neighbors.

Every now and then someone built a shed. It was the sure sign of a windfall at work.

Parents moved here to raise children. There were two or three kids in every house. Every once in a while someone accidentally bumped up to four. That was a stretch.

There were no childless couples or old people. No one lived alone. There would be no reason to move here if you wanted to be by yourself. Loneliness was allowed, but if you wanted to be alone, you had to leave.

Everyone said that if they inherited money, they would bolt to a fancier neighborhood.

We never saw a moving truck.

WHAT'S MY LINE?

Kurt wasn't the only salesman on the block. Everyone was peddling something. Everybody had a line.

Ronnie sold life insurance.

Irv sold men's big and tall clothes.

Howie sold screws.

Chip sold hot dogs with fries.

Mel, the accountant, sold tax loopholes.

Leon, the pharmacist, sold drugs.

The rabbi sold tickets to the High Holiday services. If you sat up front, you were closer to God.

LARAMIE PARK

You can go to Laramie, Wyoming. We have Laramie Park.

We lived right across the street from it. The name *Laramie* means "canopy of leafy boughs." This was aspirational. The trees were our age. They were skinny and didn't canopy anything.

The park was not a nature preserve. But it had grass. It was also a sports haven with a baseball diamond, a basketball court, and an ice-skating rink.

I thought I was the quarterback in the family, but Lenie could throw a perfect spiral. She had me running patterns before I became a receiver.

While Lenie and I were tossing a football around, we could see our dad doing figure eights on his toes, like a ballerina.

SAP

My dad planted a small sapling in the front yard. He carved Nancy's initials on the bark. They barely fit.

Lenie, Nancy, and I circled the tree when we chased fireflies on the lawn at night. To the gods, it must have looked like an archaic rite.

————

SKOKIE PREHISTORIC

In the beginning were the Mound Builders. All that's left of them are traces in the ground, remnants of chipped stone, broken tools, flattened signal towers.

HISTORY OF A VILLAGE (1)

Skokey is a Potawatomi word for "marsh." We arrived there because the Potawatomi were forcibly moved west in the 1830s. We lived a block away from Niles Center Road, which started out as an Indian trail.

The Skokie River was a wet prairie. The Potawatomi called the marshy depression *Kitchi-wap choku*. This was designated as *Chewab Skokie* on early maps. Their settlements date to the seventeenth century.

The Potawatomi were part of the Council of Three Fires, a peace alliance with the Ojibwa and Ottawa tribes. The Ojibwa were Keepers of the Faith, the Ottawa were Keepers of the Trade, and the Potawatomi were Keepers of the Sacred Fire.

The tribe consisted of farmers and medicine men. The flame-keepers had good relations with French traders, who wanted their fur, not their farmland.

The Potawatomi named it *Chicaugou* or "the Wild Onion." They called themselves *Neshnabek* or "the True People." But after the untrue people peeled the onion, the True People left in tears.

The United States government compelled the Potawatomi to cede five million acres of land in the 1833 Treaty of Chicago. After that, they lived on a reservation outside Council Bluffs, Iowa.

The Potawatomi were forced to sign forty-four treaties with the US government between 1789 and 1867. They were all lousy, but ours was probably the worst.

HISTORY OF A VILLAGE (2)

The marshland north of Chicago was resettled in the 1840s and '50s by German and Luxembourger farmers. They came from the same part of the world as my father's family. He had no idea he was following his people. He thought he was escaping them.

Farmer Harms, who founded the village, came from Mecklenburg, which was 750 kilometers from Mannheim, where my dad was born.

Niles was incorporated as a township in 1850. The town was named for Hezekiah Niles, the deceased publisher/editor of *The Niles Weekly Register,* which had gone out of business. There are eight villages, towns, and cities named Niles in the United States.

The original settlement, at Waukegan, Milwaukee, and Touhy, was a short drive from our house. We passed by it all the time, but there was nothing to mark the spot. We had no idea what we were passing. Sometimes my dad stopped for gas.

Niles Centre was incorporated as a village in 1888. Niles Township did not have a downtown, so the village claimed centrality.

Woodrow Wilson asserted, "The history of a nation is only a history of its villages written large" (*The Course of American History,* 1895). I wonder if he believed it. This was before he got the idea for the League of Nations.

No one was trying to make history. Visitors came to the village for its greenhouses, vegetable farms, and saloons, not in that order. Flowers and green beans go better with moonshine.

Merchants loved market days, which took place twice a month, and so did horse traders, beggars, fortune tellers, children, and thieves.

In those days, the Skokie Marsh north of Main Street was a haven for horse thieves. It was rumored that Cook County had more cattle rustlers than Texas and Wyoming.

The Engine House on Floral Avenue was the first public building. It had a dance hall and a jail cell. If you got too rowdy, they waltzed you from one spot to the other.

A group of upper-class Chicago businessmen founded The Links of Skokie Country Club, in 1897, but the golf course has always been in Glencoe, an older, more exclusive, clubbier suburb.

At the turn of the century, 529 people lived in the village. There was one policeman.

HISTORY OF A VILLAGE (3)

In 1903, the Chicago & North Western Railway laid down an iron trail and Niles Centre became one of the streetcar suburbs on the North Shore. Old settlers arrived in wagons. Young ones traveled on trains.

Starting in 1905, there were lots of shoot-'em-up cowboy-and-Indian movies filmed in the downtown area. It still looked like a western.

Money before death. The Niles Centre State Bank (1907) was founded six years before Memorial Park Cemetery (1913). They're both still open for business.

On a windy market day in 1910, a fire started in a barn behind Melzer's Saloon and destroyed half the business district. It took five fire departments to save the other half.

Volunteer bucket brigades and volunteer policemen fought the fire and the looters.

The drought was nationwide. Our Big Fire was small compared to the Great Fire of 1910, the Big Blowup that burned three million acres across the Northwest. That was one of the largest fires in American history.

HISTORY OF A VILLAGE (4)

In 1910, the community leaders Americanized the spelling of Niles Centre to Niles Center. RE: reversing the letters *re* wasn't enough.

Real-estate developers still didn't like the old-fashioned name because it conjured up country stores and country bumpkins. They didn't like farmland either. They wanted it paved.

Q: What happens when you put a village called Niles Center next to a village called Niles?

A: Postal confusion.

Niles was once called Dutchman's Point because the Americans didn't know the difference between the Dutch and the Germans (Deutsch).

There were sixty-one speakeasies in Niles Center during the Prohibition era (1920–1933).

Old man Haben had sturdy horses that could pull a hearse down a dirt road. He started a funeral home in 1923, and the family has been taking care of death ever since.

The first building permit went to a gas station on Niles Center Road.

My dad liked to play nine holes at the Billy Caldwell Golf Course in Forest Glen, which was founded in 1925. We didn't know it was once named Caldwell's Reservation or that Billy Caldwell was a Métis called Chief Sauganash, who negotiated the Second Treaty of Prairie du Chien with the US government, one more awful deal for the Potawatomi people.

Elevated tracks from Chicago created a real-estate boom. From 1923 to 1926 the village annexed enough land to grow from one (square mile) to ten (square miles). It maxed out when it hit the edge of seven different municipalities.

In the 1930s the boom went bust. The developers hadn't reckoned with an economic catastrophe. Skokie became a ghost town, like other American suburbs, such as Burbank, California.

There was a long string of empty streets, vacant lots. Developers used them when they started to populate the grid in the 1950s with people who wanted to own their own homes, like my folks.

HISTORY OF A VILLAGE (5)

The Bronx Building was constructed in 1927 to attract new business to Dempster Street. It cost $170,000. I liked to run up and down the marble staircase, but no one used it during the Depression. The Methodists met on the first floor until they moved to a log cabin on Concord Lane.

Why the Bronx? Because, the owner, Armond King, said, Niles Center is to Chicago as the Bronx is to Manhattan. He didn't point out that we had a semipro team, the Niles Center Indians, and they got the New York Yankees, the Bronx Bombers.

On October 29, 1929, otherwise known as Black Tuesday, Wall Street crashed, and the Great Depression began for everyone but the Niles Center Park District, which purchased sixty-two acres of land for $62,000 from the Cook County Forest Preserves.

Families were going broke, but why not lift the kids' spirits with a Boy Scout troop (1929) and a Girl Scout troop (1930)?

In 1930, a women's group called The Cosmos Club started a public library on the second floor of the Blameuser Building. The first floor rented to the Niles Center State Bank. For ten hours a week, it was books above money.

During the Depression, the bank failed and went into receivership. It later reopened as the First National Bank of Skokie. The library failed and reopened in the Municipal Building.

In 1934, a naked body wrapped in a blanket was dumped in a ditch on Niles Center Road next to St. Peter's Catholic Cemetery. This was Lester Gillis, aka Baby Face Nelson, who liked to be called Big George. We drove by the cemetery all the time, but Ruby didn't take us to pay respects because the notorious gangster wasn't buried there. He was buried in a different Catholic cemetery in River Grove.

In 1935, Tessville changed its name to Lincolnwood. Poor

Johann Tess, there were too many speakeasies in his Ville. People wanted to settle in a Wood, like Lake Forest.

Morton Grove, our neighbor to the west, is named after a railroad financier, Levi Parsons Morton, and a small group of trees.

Nothing turns on a developer like fake bucolic.

Nature needed to be protected, forests preserved. From 1933 to 1940 a new natural landscape was created from Camp Skokie Valley. This is the Skokie Lagoons.

The folks in Cook County knew how to divert a waterway. The seven artificial lagoons were established in Glencoe and Winnetka. They had better bluffs. The place was a haven for flycatchers and cuckoos.

HISTORY OF A VILLAGE (6)

On November 15, 1940, Niles Center changed its name to Skokie. More than one thousand names had been submitted. The name committee rejected Oakton, Ridgemoor, Westridge, and Woodridge. Folks wanted to live in the "Gateway to the Skokie Valley." They forgot it was built on swampland.

American amnesia: no one minded borrowing a tribal name for stolen tribal land. They didn't like to remember it was stolen. The high-school mascot was an Indian.

The Skokie flag was green with two vertical yellow stripes. It showed the founding date, 1888, and an Indian chief in profile. He couldn't bear to look straight ahead.

The postwar boom was on. Time to rezone. In 1946, the Skokie Village master plan called for dumping apartments and constructing single-family residences.

The small houses bloomed in rows. The lots were narrow and there were lots of them.

To spur sales, the developers advertised in gritty Jewish neighborhoods on the South, West, and North Sides. They would have carpeted the East Side, too, but that's a lake.

The message was clear: "Sick of the city? Want to escape to suburbia? We're not scared of you."

The last piece of the puzzle was the car. "Want to drive between Chicago and Skokie? We'll get you rolling."

William Grant Edens was a pioneer of pavement in the mud-ridden state of Illinois. His Eden was concrete from the ground up. Edens Parkway opened in 1951. It was Chicago's first expressway.

The plot worked 300 percent. Build a house and a highway and they, I mean we, will come. In 1959, my family lifted the population from 59,359 to 59,364. Fifty-eight percent of the population was Jewish. About 7,500 were Holocaust survivors. No one realized the place was founded by Germans. We might have known. It's a ten-mile square grid.

European history seemed far away. But every now and then, you glimpsed someone with a number tattooed on his arm walking home with a bag of bialys.

On the census, the survivors didn't know what to mark. My parents checked *White*.

HISTORY OF A VILLAGE (7)

Skokie now had a village manager, a court of record, and a middle-aged mayor who taught accounting at Northwestern University in Evanston.

Everyone we knew commuted to work. No one commuted together. The mayor was in the minority because most people drove to Chicago.

It was short-sighted for Skokie to bill itself "Village of Vision." The trustees dropped the slogan when they discovered we had more residents than Oak Park.

In 1962, Skokie proclaimed itself "the World's Largest Village." I checked the stats. We were neck and neck with Baniachong in Bangladesh.

13

BACK TO THE LAND

We were a world away from Hacker's farm stand near Touhy and Niles Center Road. You crossed the road from Laramie Park to a homestead with greenhouses.

If you had a nickel, you could scoop Orange Crush from an ice chest. There was a bottle opener attached to its side.

I thought a workhorse was a person who worked hard. I didn't know there were real workhorses who neighed and stomped on the ground.

I slipped in to walk around the barn. I didn't know there was such a thing as truck farming. This was our last tangible remnant of the country in the suburb. There was land under our feet.

OLD ORCHARD

The Old Orchard Center opened on eighty-five acres in 1956. It was neither old nor an orchard, but there was plenty of open-air parking on land that had once been a prairie filled with water.

The mall was manufactured by American Community Builders. Its name was homespun, the company not.

The center of the Center was Marshall Field & Company. The mall had a second anchor, the Fair Store, which was later rebranded as Montgomery Ward, and more than one million leasable square feet.

The mall was a cluster-type shopping center. There was a five-and-dime, a drug store, and a supermarket. The underground concourse housed an Arcade Barber Shop, an Arcade Currency

Exchange, and an Arcade Travel Bureau. You could get your haircut, change your money, and see the world from the basement.

The real goods were upstairs. Old Orchard was a new kind of market town within the village, a natural place to shop.

GOLF MILL

Not to be outdone, Golf Mill Center opened in neighboring Niles in 1960. Built on eighty-eight acres of farmland, it had a real fake mill with a working waterwheel, ponds, and bridges. The office tower looked like the top of a golf ball. From up there, the mall looked like a miniature golf course.

LANDMARKS

In the nineteenth century, Henry (Heinrich) Harms built a plank toll road along Little Fort Trail so my family could drive down Lincoln Avenue to a new home. The tollgates were long gone.

Emerson Street was named after Benjamin, not Ralph Waldo, Chicago's first milkman. We were self-reliant—no one got milk delivered anymore.

The Leaning Tower of Niles was half a mile from our house. Who cared if it was only half the size of the Tower of Pisa? It was 4,642.5 miles closer. And it was building a Y.

Abraham Lincoln had lots of log cabins, but there was only one Elliott's Pine Log Restaurant and Lounge.

Parker's Drugstore sported a soda fountain where you downed Green River. It was mobbed on St. Patrick's Day when everyone wanted green pop.

Mr. Rickey's was named after the owner's kid at the cash register. He hated his nickname, and everyone called him Rich.

Kaufman's Deli was a nerve center for survivors. The smoked fish and thick accents had Old World flavor. You could get a nosh and an insult in five or six languages.

You had to cross the bridge over Edens Expressway to get to downtown Skokie. There was only a small dirt path past an elementary school. You felt like a trailblazer. No one else walked to the center.

There was a small hill next to the highway where we went sledding. We had a red Flexible Flyer sled and a silver flying saucer. You skidded down the hill into the street. It was just you, your sled, and cars sliding by in the snow.

The gateway to downtown Skokie was a giant sign that gave the okay to buy used cars at Mancuso Chevrolet.

If you're Catholic, you go to one St. Peter's. If you're Protestant, you go to the other.

In 1867, Peter Blameuser Jr. donated land for both Peters. He was ecumenical, but everyone thought he was a saint.

"Behold, how good and how pleasant *it is* for brethren to live together in unity!" (Psalm 133:1). But then Lutheran St. Paul split from Lutheran St. Peter and a new church was built in 1881. This was Skokie's third-oldest church, but some folks were still fuming about it.

There were Reform, Conservative, and Orthodox synagogues, but my mom thought they were déclassé.

The Hebrew Theological College, otherwise known as the Skokie Yeshiva, scorned the secular. But those guys went hard to the hoop on the basketball court behind school. Their kippahs were pinned to their hair and tzitzis flew around their shirts.

If you missed the bus, you had to run across Touhy to get to Fairview South Elementary School. It was a major thoroughfare, and there was no stoplight. It seemed like playing dodgeball with speeding cars. You didn't want to get tagged.

Fairview School opened in 1858. It took 102 years for us to get there. Its new district was founded in 1950. That only took ten years. But it was my entire life.

———

ON BEING BLUE

My friend Layf lived down the street from school on Fairview Lane. His whole house was decorated sky blue. You walked on a carpet of blue sea. You gazed up at a ceiling of blue sky.

Layf's grandfather owned Abbot Paints. They named it that so they would be first in the phone book. His great-uncle Bernie was the interior decorator for the company. He was the fancy one in the family. He had a Blue Period, like Picasso.

Years later I studied with the fiction writer William Gass, who was trained as a philosopher. He wrote a meditation called *On Being Blue*. I had to break it to him that Uncle Bernie thought of it first.

Layf's father, Seymour, was a lawyer. His practice did not include smiling. He threatened to sue you if you stepped on his perfectly manicured lawn. I cut our grass. Seymour had a service.

Layf's mother, Betty, was better tempered. She bought boxes of Good Humor. You could get Strawberry Shortcake and Chocolate Éclair bars from the coolest refrigerator on Fairview Lane. It was light blue.

UPWARD MOBILITY

The houses were bigger on the other side of Fairview School. You moved there if you were a doctor or a lawyer. The kids' parents were professional. Ours were un.

I can still reel off the streets like the Cubs infield. When the grownups weren't around, you could toss a ball from Lunt to Coyle to Morse to Farwell.

Pratt was the last avenue in Skokie. It was a busy pinnacle where you crossed over into Lincolnwood. You felt like a trespasser because there were no sidewalks. There were full-grown trees the color of freshly made money.

KIDDIELAND

The rich kids had their birthday parties at Hollywood Kiddieland. You got picked up in a Kiddie fire truck and rode around the park on a mini train. If you were gutsy, you mounted the Wild Mouse. One kid from East Prairie was starstruck. He wanted to be buried under the Little Dipper.

BOUNCE LAND

If you had generous friends, their parents brought you to the Lincoln Devon Bounce Land. It cost them fifty cents to jump on a trampoline for half an hour. It was fun until kids started falling off and hurting themselves. Then lawsuits bounced Bounce Land out of existence.

———

HOUSE IN WILMETTE

Auntie Bea and Uncle Bob moved to Wilmette before we moved to Skokie. They had a smaller house, but it was in a ritzier suburb. I asked my aunt why we didn't move there too. She said, "Your mother never wanted to follow me."

Bea inherited my grandmother's gene for cleaning. She vacuumed diagonally. The carpet looked like a pristine beach. It was as if no one ever walked on it.

This was saying something because Bea had three kids: Mickey, Allan, and Barbie. These were our true cousins in wildness. This was blood and blood ain't pee. You laughed with them in the morning and cried with them at night.

STEALTH

The thing to do was to slip out of your room at night. You crawled through the hallway. You hit the ground if you heard a noise. You were silent opening a door. One by one you gathered everyone.

You muffled your voices and hid under the covers. You slithered back into bed at dawn. No one knew the difference. But you left tracks. Auntie Bea always knew you had been up because the carpet was ruffled.

SWELL

Uncle Bob had a construction business that seemed a bit wobbly. But he knew how to build a house. He knew how to furnish one too because he installed a ping pong table and a pinball machine in their basement. You could go downstairs to ping and plonk for hours. You didn't have to pay to replay.

Uncle Bob was the only adult who really talked to us. He wanted to hear our opinions. He was good at debating and ping pong. We didn't care if he was a developer who never emotionally developed. He took an interest.

But Uncle Bob was too cocky. One summer he got his thumb caught in a lawn mower. It was malformed. He had a swollen hand to go with his swelled head.

Bob wanted to be a pro bowler. Now he couldn't control the ball with his thumb. His average plummeted. If he wanted to mow down pins, he never should have mowed the lawn.

AUNT SANDY AND UNCLE PETER DROVE DOWN
FROM KENOSHA, WISCONSIN

Uncle Bob's sister, Sandy, was the less-favored child. Her parents criticized her constantly. She was a substitute schoolteacher who talked and talked. She could empty a room. She drank too much. It was hard to blame her, though, because she was married to Peter.

Uncle Peter was in waste management. My dad was the only one who liked him. He was tall and undistinguished except for his sense of humor. He loved cruelty. He was gleeful when someone suffered a heart attack at the Oscar Mayer plant. He was excited when a cat got electrocuted on a cable behind his house. He would pop out photographs of gruesome murders and laugh out loud.

SICK HUMOR

We heard rumors that Uncle Peter had been in a concentration camp somewhere in Eastern Europe. He came by his sick humor honestly.

CARTOONS

Uncle Bob's cousin Julie was married to Ronnie, who was the art director at a magazine. He was the only person I knew who could truly draw. I considered him a realist because he made all the adults look like cartoon characters.

HONORARY

Julie and Ronnie had three kids: David, Darryl, and Gregg. We treated them as honorary cousins. Their house was a neutral zone, like Switzerland. We didn't belong there, but it was peaceful, and the chocolates were top-notch.

ALL OUR FAKE AUNTS AND UNCLES

spread out and moved to the suburbs, too. They came piling over on Sundays from their new houses in Lincolnwood and Winnetka, which they could afford, or they couldn't afford. Banks were involved. People drank Bloody Marys and screwdrivers. There were whispers in the corner. Someone was always on top, someone else in arrears.

NIECES AND NEPHEWS, NOT COUSINS

Our uncles and aunts had kids. Two and three apiece. My mother loved those kids and doted on them as family. They called her Auntie Irma and came to our parties. But we were never close to them. We waved and moved on. We never considered them cousins.

NEIGHBORS

Our house was nine feet away from the house next door. From my bedroom window I could see Alex and Edith in their room at night. She had red beehive hair and looked like the female lead in *The Bride of Frankenstein.* He looked like a schlub. They were constantly arguing. It was like watching an old movie with the sound turned off. I couldn't decide if it was funny or sad.

My dad had a salesman's personality. He liked to chat with the neighbors, but he didn't make friends with anyone.

My mom made friends with Yudi and Sissy. We drew the line and refused to call them Aunt Yudi and Aunt Sissy. They were married to Irv and Ron. They were not uncles.

Yudi had the gift for gab. She had the gruff voice of a chain smoker. She lived in the fourth house of our block. I never heard her at a loss for words. She didn't pause to take a breath. If you tried to interrupt her, she got louder and talked over you.

Sissy lived in the third house. She was a good talker too. But she couldn't keep up—she didn't have the stamina. Sometimes she'd fall silent. When Yudi and Irv moved to Indianapolis, Sissy began to shine. There were no silent pauses. In no time at all, she became the number-one talker on our block.

I WONDER WHAT FREUD WOULD SAY

On Sunday morning, my dad bought bagels at New York Bagel & Bialy. My mom used a little guillotine to cut them in half.

SUNDAY BRUNCH

There were more people than my mom expected at Sunday brunch. She pulled Lenie and me aside. "Don't eat anything until you see if there is enough food." We waited until everyone helped themselves. There was more than enough. There was so much food that my mom sent some of it home with the guests.

FAMILY OF OVEREATERS

We did not stop but barreled past Go. Overeating was a Ginsburg and Rubenstein specialty. It was not a Hirsch trait. Perhaps I should make an exception for my dad's brother, Harry. He was on our side.

LAST COURSE

There were too many desserts at my mother's parties. She took a Blakean approach to the end of a meal: "The road of excess leads to the palace of wisdom."

SERVING SPOON

"Use a spoon," my father said. "I don't know where those hands have been."

THE GINSBURG PICK

My father called it *the Ginsburg pick*. He believed that you should cut a piece of cake and eat it. My grandmother, my mother, and my aunt disagreed. The idea was to leave the cake on the table. You never had to take a piece. You never ate it. You just picked at it until the cake was finished.

Years later I told my grandmother that my my graduate school friend Amy had written an article on portion control. She called it "The Ginsburg Pick." My grandma said that she picked up the habit from her mother, Malka. Amy should have used her mother's maiden name. It could have been called "The Pochapovsky Pick."

I asked Lenie if Ruby and Beverly liked the leftover pick too. She didn't know if they were picky. We couldn't remember eating at their place.

ON LA CROSSE

Ruby and Beverly lived on La Crosse Avenue on the other side of Skokie. They rented a co-op down the street from an undertaker.

Ruby wanted to get out of there and drove too fast. The neighborhood was once called Sharp Corner.

Lenie and I were like French explorers. Sometimes we played on the first paved concrete road in Skokie. This was Church Street. We tried to rile everyone up by telling them we went to church on Saturday.

STEPFAMILY

We couldn't figure out how to feel about Beverly's family. They were step, but not very. We just called everyone Aunt and Uncle for convenience, like her older sister, Annabel, and her brother-in-law, Raymie. She was a pianist who accompanied her father and brother in synagogue. He was an Insurance Adjustor of the crooked variety.

It seemed better not to tell our mom about all the extras, but she knew them anyway growing up in the neighborhood. They were not the problem. The problem was the high-school sweetheart she had married and divorced.

ARCHIMEDES AND UNCLE RAYMIE

Archimedes discovered his theory of displacement by standing in a bathtub. We learned it when Uncle Raymie jumped into the swimming pool and splashed out half the water.

Eureka! We knew Uncle Raymie was big and beefy. We didn't

know he was bald until his toupee sank slowly to the bottom of the pool.

HALF-SIBLINGS

Ruby and Beverly smelted us a half brother named Ellis. He had his mother's love and his father's scrap. Emperor Ellis was destined for Empire Metals.

Three months later Beverly was pregnant with Queen Helen. But we were no longer around when our half sister was born.

A FAVORITE WORD

Zugzwang means the same thing in life as it does in chess. You need to move, but every move makes the situation worse.

14

NAME CHANGE

When we moved to Skokie, our mother changed our last name to Hirsch. She said it was better for a family to have one name. It never occurred to us to question her.

Ruby found out when we showed him our report cards from Fairview School. We were proud of our good grades. He said, "What's this?"

For a moment, he looked stunned. Then he started yelling at us.

WHAT'S IN A NAME?

I don't recall anyone ever calling me *Edward Rubenstein*. Yet that was my name until I was nine years old. Lenie can't remember anyone calling her *Arlene Rubenstein* either. We blocked it. Teachers must have called us Rubenstein all the time. Maybe a name is something that you take for granted as a kid. It's just there, like the weather. But then the weather changes dramatically. One moment you're walking in sunlight, the next you're caught in a storm.

THE LAWSUIT

Ruby was suing your mother, he was suing you, about your last name. The two of you would run it down in your heads. You were sticking together no matter what, Rubenstein or Hirsch, Hirsch or Rubenstein, Rubenstein-Hirsch, Hirsch-Rubenstein. It sounded like a jump-rope game. You were the jumpers.

A CHESS GAME

We are watching from the stairs. Ruby and Irma are sitting in the living room talking about other things. No one raises a voice. They are ice calm. Imagine a chess game between the Russians and the Americans during the Cold War. No one flinches. Kids are pawns.

THE THERAPIST IN EVANSTON

Someone opened a copy of *Grimms' Fairy Tales* and an old man with a beard stepped out. He lived at the top of crooked stairs in a wooden house. He spoke with an accent and gave strange tests with ink blots that you could not pass or fail.

RORSCHACH TEST

I saw a butterfly, a baseball bat, and an elephant trunk. Lenie saw Bucky's penis.

NORMALITY

"The psychiatrist gave me his evaluation," my mom said, "and you two are totally normal."

She could get us to accept some real whoppers, but this one was too hard to believe.

OUR DAY IN COURT

We're in City Hall. Everyone is dressed up. There are lots of kids in the hallway, but no one is playing, and they all look miserable.

Suddenly, a clerk shouts "Rubenstein-Hirsch," and we file into family court. Lenie and are lined up at one table with our mom. Ruby is sitting at another table by himself. There is an aisle between us. It is wider than the Chicago River. We all stand for the judge.

We are scared of the man in the long black robe who calls us into his chambers. He wants us to decide our last name. We have no idea whether to choose mother or father. They are sitting on the other side of the door.

I suggest we use both names. The judge shakes his head. This is not possible.

He turns to my sister, who turns to me. She says, "I'll take whatever name he takes."

The judge scowls at the papers on his desk. He looks upset. He mutters something unintelligible.

We trudge back to the table. Our mom goes into the chamber. We sit there fidgeting until she comes out. Then Ruby goes into the chamber, too. It takes a long time.

We are leaving the courtroom. The judge has ruled.

SOMETHING HARD TO FORGET

We parked outside the house on Sherwin Avenue. Ruby was sitting in the driver's seat. Lenie and I huddled in the back seat. We sobbed hysterically. Our father had lost the court case to change our last name back to Rubenstein. That's why he was moving to California. "I never want to see you again!" he shouted at us. "You're traitors! You're not my children anymore! Forget I ever existed! From now on, you're dead to me!"

ALL ROADS LEAD TO ABANDONMENT

We cried, "If you don't want to see us, we don't want to see you either!"

Ruby drove off. He told Beverly about it later. "Can you believe it?" he complained. "They said they never wanted to see me again."

———

WINTER IN CHICAGO

"Poor Harold," Beverly said. "Irma has them brainwashed. His own children don't want to see him. What can we do about it?"

Now that she was a mother, Beverly realized that winter in Chicago is hazardous. Ellis was learning to walk, Helen to crawl. She was skidding their buggies on ice. They were sliding around the back seat of the car.

Beverly had an idea from her former Beverly life. They could start over with two babies in the Golden State. They could raise golden replacement children.

There was one problem with the plan: Harold's gambling.

TWO WIVES, ONE ADDICTION

When we came home from school, Beverly was sitting in the living room with our mom. Helen was crawling around on the carpet. Beverly had come to ask her opinion on whether she should leave Ruby because of his gambling.

Irma and Beverly used to be friends. Then Irma and Harold got divorced. Then Beverly and Harold met and married. Then Irma and Beverly stopped being friends. But Irma could still give a consult. She knew something about Harold.

"True story," my mom said. "Beverly keeps asking me whether or not she should leave Ruby."

Whenever my mom said "true story," we knew that the story might not be true. But Auntie Bea confirmed this one.

HIGH STAKES

Uncle Itchy warned Beverly, "You can't control him." This was true. A gambler needs to play over his head for it to be exciting. Sometimes he wagers the family. Ruby lost the first round, won the second.

BUSTED

When he left us standing on the sidewalk, Ruby didn't tell us that he had lost his metal yard. He had bet uncontrollably. The problem was not cards. The commodity copper market took him down. But we didn't go down with him. We went down without him.

ADVERTISEMENT FOR ABANDONMENT

Ruby and Beverly moved to LA. Ruby refused to give us up for adoption. A lawyer told my mother what to do. She put an advertisement for abandonment in the Chicago papers. Ruby didn't see it. He couldn't respond. A year passed. Legally, he wasn't our father anymore. Kurt was free to adopt us.

CASE WITHDRAWN

Lenie and I spent most of our lives believing that we knew what happened with our court case. No one told us otherwise.

We were in our sixties when Beverly mentioned in passing that she had pressed Ruby to pursue the lawsuit over our last name. He was a reluctant plaintiff. But she was righteous and stoked his rage.

Beverly also let it slip that Ruby never really lost the case. Instead, the judge convinced him to withdraw it altogether. It had nothing to do with legal merit. He argued that the fight was screwing us up. We were troubled.

Ruby was furious about his decision. He felt the court had forced his hand. Therefore, he never told us. He wanted us to believe it was our fault.

My mom didn't tell us either. She never conceded that Ruby had dropped the case. She wanted us to believe that her rash decision to change our last name was legally justified even though it was not.

She also wanted us to blame our natural father for blaming us. She got her way there, too.

THE VAULT

Fifty years later my wife Laurie and I took my mother to the bank. She was suffering from dementia. She wanted to check the vault.

While my mom counted CDs, Laurie leafed through papers. "Hey, Hershey, look at this," she said. "Check the date."

It was the document for my name change. My mother did not

change my name when I was ten years old. That was a cover story. She changed it the night before I turned twenty-one.

Here were the adoption papers to prove it. I was not adopted at the age of ten. That was something to tell children. I was adopted when I came of age.

THE STORYTELLER

When we were teenagers, my mother got us social security cards and passports with the name Hirsch. She had no backing, no proof. The case had been withdrawn. Legally, our name was still Rubenstein. She turned on the charm. She convinced people. My sister and I weren't just irregulars. We were also illegals.

FROM THE ARCHIVE OF FAMILY SECRETS

My parents did not tell Nancy that she had a different father than Lenie and me. She knew something was off-kilter. She decided that she had been adopted.

Nancy was in high school when she figured out that she was not adopted. Kurt was her natural father. She was surprised, however, to discover that he was not our natural father. We were adopted.

ON THE BRIDGE

I was going over the story again. I sighed, "It's all water under the bridge now."

Laurie said, "Yes, Hershey, but you're still standing on that bridge."

———

NEW PACKAGING

In California, Ruby and Beverly had another family to worry about. They were flat broke. They lived with Aunt Becky in an adult-only building. The parents slept in the living room. The kids slept in the bedroom with Becky. This was not the Beverly life Beverly envisioned.

Aunt Becky never let the children cry. She was afraid she'd get kicked out of her building. Harold yelled, "You're seventy-nine years old for Chrissake! No one is going to evict you. Everyone here loves the kids."

Becky didn't listen. She thought Harold was childish.

Ruby told Beverly he had a job as a scale man at a scrap yard. This was the truth scaled back. It lasted one day.

Ruby told Beverly he was selling pots and pans door-to-door. She never saw a pot or a pan. He was playing poker at the Normandie Club in Gardena.

Ruby couldn't believe his good luck. Poker was a game of skill. They proved it in court. Poker clubs were legal.

It was a twenty-minute drive from downtown LA to the lushest garden spot on the West Coast. My delinquent father had landed in a suburb of paradise, otherwise known as the Poker Capital of the World. It had six clubs.

Gamblers are superstitious. Ruby liked the four-leaf clover in front of the Normandie. But whenever his luck turned, he switched to the Rainbow or the Horseshoe. He liked their signs, too.

Ruby brought home his new buddies. They dealt from the bottom of the deck; they outdid each other with card tricks. The house was filled with anglers and hustlers.

Ruby's Aunt Sadie intervened. She said, "My Arthur will give Harold a job. He's a big man. He gives everyone a job."

Arthur was a visionary. He went from the paper-box business to skin packaging.

Ruby went to work for Arthur in the packaging business. The big man gave the little man the worst neighborhoods. Ruby didn't care. He knew where to drive, what to do. He was a salesman. Salesmen sell.

Ruby scored a large deal with a shoe-polishing company. He could see the future. It was Bubble Wrap.

Bubble Wrap gave Ruby a big stake. He used it to play poker at the Normandie.

GAM-ANON

Beverly decided to join Gam-Anon. She went to meetings. She had a sponsor. One night they took Ruby to dinner. The sponsor made his pitch. Ruby balked. "I am not ready for Gamblers Anonymous." But the next day he got a job as a foreman for Alpert & Alpert.

ALPERT & ALPERT

Ruby went back to basic training. He learned scrap from the ground up. He got dirty. Every night Beverly sprayed him down with a hose. Then the family headed to the beach.

Ruby refused to tip the scales for anyone. He wouldn't upgrade the metals. One guy kept trying to pay him off. Ruby told him to get off the lot. Instead, he tried to run Ruby over with his truck.

Someone tried to kill Ruby who was not my mother.

Ruby pulled the crook out of the cab and slugged him. The Alpert brothers would have looked the other way, but their mother was on the premises. Frida said, "As much as we love you, you can't hit a customer no matter what." Ruby got fired.

Ruby failed forward. He got fit. He started playing gin rummy at the Encino Health Club in the San Fernando Valley.

FOUR CHILDREN

Ellis and Helen grew up on the west side of Los Angeles. They played in the sun. Lenie and I grew up on the North Side of Chicago. We played in the snow.

Lenie and I didn't think much of Ellis and Helen. They didn't think of us at all because no one told them we existed.

Harold did not know the originals. He knew the replacements.

When we were grown up, Ruby told us, "I will always love Ellis and Helen better than you, because I raised them."

Ruby knew what it meant not to raise children. He had a loose interpretation of what it meant to raise them.

15

THE ITALIAN PALAZZO

My mother had a vision. The tract house in Skokie was meant to resemble an Italian palazzo. When you walked through the front door, you were greeted by a wallpaper image of a Roman villa overlooking the living room. It was move-in ready for an emperor like Hadrian or a movie star like Cary Grant.

DRESSING THE PART

My mom had two sets of hostess gowns.

Every night she came home and cooked in a velour gown that zipped up the front. She wanted us to dress up for dinner. We refused.

My dad wore a sport coat and tie to work. He came home and put on a tee shirt and baggy pants.

My mother wore a two-piece peignoir to bed. She slept in a silk nightgown. My dad slept in boxer shorts.

My mom wore an elegant velvet hostess gown to receive company. She couldn't convince my dad to wear a smoking jacket.

THE LIVING ROOM

was off-limits to the family. The deep white shag carpet was untouched.

The couch was apricot velvet. Plastic slipcovers only came off for company. They wheezed and stuck to you when you sat on them.

There was a round marble coffee table, a pink silk-striped love-seat, and a painting of sailboats on a clear blue lake. It was framed in gold gilt.

The heavy ivory damask drapes were closed so no one could see the street.

The centerpiece was a baby grand piano that my mom bought from Shirley Klipp for twenty-five bucks. It made the downscale trip from Lake Shore Drive to Niles Township.

My mom had a fantasy of her girls in long dresses playing concerts on Sunday afternoons. The piano was out of tune. No one played.

PHANTOM CLOCK

For decades I recalled a broken grandfather clock that stood guarding the front hall like a sentinel. My sisters said it didn't exist and was never there. It was a screen memory. It screened out time.

THE DINING ROOM

The terrazzo floor was dirty. But the chips of marble, quartz, and glass made it hard to tell that my mother never changed the water in the bucket when she mopped. The room was filled by a polished wooden table that could be extended for company. The wax fruit in a bowl never ripened or rotted. It stayed there unchanging year after year.

THE GIANT MIRROR

My sisters shared a bedroom. The centerpiece was a giant mirror with a long marble shelf where the girls were supposed to sit on a royal-blue bench and put on makeup for years at a time.

MANICURE SCISSORS

Lenie ran when she saw my mom coming with manicure scissors. My mom raced after her to cut Lenie's bangs. She caught her. That's why Lenie's bangs were always crooked. They curved like the blade. Nancy was too young to run away. Her bangs were crooked too. They looked like the Bobbsey Twins with sketchy haircuts.

NIGHT CONVERSATION

The pole in Lenie's closet kept collapsing. Her clothes landed in a heap on the floor. Our closets were connected by a thin wall. She sat on her sweaters and talked to me through plaster.

THE REC ROOM

was not a smashing success. It had a small bar and a working fireplace. But no one used the bar or built a fire. There was a round table to play games, but no one played games. My dad hosted a weekly gin game. They gathered in the kitchen.

ESCAPE HATCH

You could climb out the window in the rec room and go to the park across the street, but you had to make sure to wipe away your footprints when you got home. My dad checked for prowlers. My mom often forgot her keys. She backed in through the window. This was awkward. She left big clumps of dirt on the windowsill. My dad never suspected her. He grilled each of us in turn. We never squealed. She didn't raise rats.

FLOOD

We lived at the bottom of a street where the rainwater ran downhill. Our basement flooded whenever it rained hard. There was a sump pump in the crawl space, but it was hard to reach. We didn't get to it in time. When the downpour started, we piled up the furniture on the bar. We sloshed around in our boots.

AFTER THE DELUGE

It was not a good idea to walk barefoot in the basement. There were water bugs scattered across the wet floor. Once Lenie had a sleepover. All the girls were talking in the basement when the water bugs appeared. The girls ran upstairs screaming.

LIBRARY

There was an extra room in the basement my mom called *the library*. It didn't have many books in it.

The library was damp. The paperbacks curled in protest. If you had a book that you cared about, you kept it in your room.

My parents had a water-damaged copy of *The Power of Positive Thinking*. No one read it. The power was supposed to come to you through osmosis.

The book was missing its front cover. I opened it to a line that began, "The trouble with most of us." The rest of the sentence was blurred.

There was another line that started, "I'll tell you a secret." I never found out what the secret was.

My mom had the notion that someday my grandmother would move into the library. But whenever she brought it up my grandma pooh-poohed the idea. She was too independent to live with us. The room was moldy. Reading was a waste of time.

MICROCOSM

The laundry room was a microcosm of the family. It was everyone for themselves.

My mom had a laundry chute in her closet. She had to come clean whenever she caught her hand in it. Sometimes she walked around with a bloody bandage.

The clothes shot directly to the basement. There was no basket at the bottom. The dirty clothes pooled on the dirty concrete.

Whoever went into the room was supposed to throw in a load of laundry. The wet laundry sat in the washing machine until someone moved it to the dryer.

The clothes sat in the dryer until someone needed something. Whoever needed something piled the clean laundry on top of the dryer. The clean clothes looked down on the dirty clothes.

A lot of clean clothes fell behind the dryer. You had to crawl behind the dryer to get your stuff. It was a little dirty.

The clean clothes shed dirty tears.

OPEN REBELLION

The appliances rebel against the working conditions in the house. They go on one-day strikes. The air conditioner won't start, the refrigerator won't defrost, the dishwasher won't drain. We promise to treat them better. We plead with them to return to work. Sometimes they comply.

THE TELEPHONE

Skokie was a haven for household phones, but we couldn't get one that worked. Ours was like a family therapist. It felt we had taken dysfunction to a new level. But it was fair-minded. It didn't speak. It didn't function for everyone.

FIXING IT

My mother and I panicked whenever something broke in the house. We could not fix things. We were equal in our inability. She was older but I was a male and so our low scores evened out. I would give myself a slightly higher grade because I could change a light bulb.

THE ATHEIST

My dad was an atheist. He made a big point of it. He thought he was good at fixing stuff. That was a stretch. But he was better than the rest of us. He yelled at me when I couldn't figure out how to do things, like jump-start the car or change a flat tire. I drew a blank. The atheist said, "Concentrate. God is in the details."

DETAILS, DETAILS

My dad called me a wiseacre when I found out that the architect Mies van der Rohe took the expression "God is in the details" from a German proverb and changed it to something he liked better. My father hated Teutonic sayings. Sorry, but Mies was right: the devil is in the details, too.

THE GARBAGE DISPOSAL

"The garbage disposal is backed up."
   "No need to call a plumber. Daddy can fix it."
   "Call the plumber. Your father just made it worse."

GARBAGE

There were no garbage cans in our house. My mother thought they were unrefined. We put the garbage in a small plastic bag that hung over a drawer in the kitchen. It usually spilled over. Every couple of days we tossed it into a can in the alley.

AT THE BEACH

My mom took us to Montrose Beach with some of our friends. When she opened the paper bag to feed us, she realized that she had brought the garbage for lunch.

HAND TOWELS

There were elegant cloth hand towels in the downstairs bathroom.
They were not supposed to be used to dry your hands.

BATH TOWELS

My mother could not find a bath towel that covered more than the
front part of her body. After her bath, she ran down the hall in a
skimpy white towel. It was a short hallway. My father yelled at her
about it for forty years.

TWO CLOSETS

It was like the difference between Germany and Russia. My dad's
closet was orderly, my mother's wardrobe was a chaotic mess.

INSOMNIA

My mother did not sleep well. She did not value other people's
sleep, either. A few times a week she vacuumed the carpet at 5 a.m.
and woke everyone. She was lonely and wanted to talk.

CALL TO BREAKFAST

My mom rattled the pots and pans in the kitchen so we would
wake up. She was preparing breakfast: cold cereal.

HOME IMPROVEMENT

1.

There were goldfish swimming on the wallpaper in the down-
stairs bathroom. My mom decided to paint them green. This was
a middle-of-the-night project. Unfortunately, she wasn't good at
coloring inside the lines. In the morning, all the fish looked like
sloppy green blobs. The wallpaper needed to be replaced.

2.

One night my mom spray-painted a green ceramic elephant lamp gold. For a moment she thought she was in New Delhi.

COMEDY OF ERRORS

1.

My mother left the vacuum on the stairs to go answer the phone. Lenie tripped over it and sprained her ankle.

2.

My mom coated the bottom of the bathtub with bleach and went to talk on the phone. The bleach was Comet Cleanser. Lenie took a bath in green bleach.

3.

My mom didn't mention that she sprayed the inside of the oven with oven cleaner. Lenie popped in a pot pie. It tasted fine. But when my mom realized what had happened, she rushed Lenie to the emergency room. She did not want to poison her. Lenie drank vinegar to cleanse her system.

4.

What's in oven cleaner anyway? We looked it up. I tried not to be caustic about the fact that Lenie ate caustic soda. She vowed, "Hell will freeze over before I eat antifreeze again."

5.

When I was a freshman in high school, I read Shakespeare's *Comedy of Errors*. I didn't understand it any better than my mom's housekeeping.

SNEAK EATING

Every night my mother snuck downstairs for something to eat. My father woke up and chased after her. He found her sitting at the table drinking a glass of milk in a skimpy nightie. There was never food to be seen anywhere.

SITTING ON THE CANDY JAR

Everyone knew that my dad hid the candy in the piano bench. Whenever my mom wanted a sweet pick-me-up, she went into the living room and snuck a few pieces.

THINGAMAJIG

Nancy rigged up pots and pans to the cabinets. The doors rattled whenever you opened them. She also roped them to the refrigerator. No one could eat anything without everyone else hearing the noise. This Rube Goldberg contraption lasted one night.

THE ROAD WELL-TRAVELED

In the 1950s, my father wore house shoes to the icebox, but in the 1960s he started to wear slippers to the refrigerator. My mother went barefoot.

16

AUBADE

In our house, there was shouting in the early morning. My father yelled at my mother because she threw out the paper. My mother yelled at my father because he forgot to go to the bank. My father yelled at my mother because he had mismatched socks. My mother yelled at my father because he neglected to fix the sink. Sometimes you could overhear them on the phone during the day—it was lovey-dovey. They held hands at night.

KEYS

Every evening my dad placed his keys on the sideboard in the dining room. Every night my mother moved them.

Every morning my dad freaked out because he was late for work. He couldn't find his keys. My mom said, "Oh, Kurt, you'd lose your head if it wasn't screwed on."

The keys magically reappeared. Order was restored. The day unlocked.

COFFEE WITH CREAM AND SUGAR

My parents had an argument at breakfast. My mom got mad and poured cream on my dad's head. He retaliated by pouring sugar on her head. No one touched the hot coffee.

AT THE FIGHTS

We had ringside seats to the fights. They were all about money. It was not a complicated fight. There was not enough of it.

ON CREMATION

Our dad said that he wanted to be cremated. He did it to peeve our mother. "Oh, Kurt," she said, "cut it out. I need somewhere to go to argue with you."

MOTHERS' HELPERS

My mother founded a Mothers' Helpers agency. Every Friday in spring there were teenagers from Wisconsin and Indiana waiting in our basement. The middle-class mothers interviewed them in the living room. I loved seeing the Mothers' Helpers in our rec room. I never talked to any of them, but I felt like an explorer venturing toward enchanted territory.

SEXUAL EDUCATION

My mom worried that I would get myself in trouble with one of her Helpers. She didn't want anyone to help themselves. My dad sat down to tell me the facts of life. We were embarrassed. "Don't worry," I told him. "I know about all that." He was relieved and left. I didn't know anything about anything.

WEDDING CONSULTANT

My mom started a wedding consultant business. We were enlisted to arrange invitations and set place cards. The weddings didn't interest me, but the sweet tables were amazing. This wasn't like the Mothers' Helpers. Once everyone left, I could help myself.

IRMA OF GOODIES

My mother's one long-lasting business was her jewelry company, Irma of Goodies. She invented her own cottage industry. She never had a store. She found wholesalers on Jewelers' Row who lent her everything on consignment. She sold her merchandise in three beauty salons on Dempster Street. She sat in an empty stylist's chair and spread her stuff on a table. Women in hair curlers flocked around "the Queen of Genuine Jewelry at Discount Prices."

PARTNERSHIP

At first my mom had a partner. This was our second Aunt Edie. She was put together and wore her hair in a prim bun. But she had a loud, raspy voice that placed her in the stratosphere with Aunt Idel and Aunt Harriet.

Aunt Edie was married to Uncle Jackie, who owned a couple of gas stations on the South Side. He drove a black Cadillac and wore more jewelry than his wife.

Edie and my mom disagreed on price points. My mom knew her clientele and went low. Edie knew hers and went high.

Aunt Edie didn't need the side hustle and the partnership dissolved. She drove off in her new Cadillac to her new house in Lincolnwood.

No hard feelings. Aunt Edie and Uncle Jackie came to all my mom's parties. They were fancy fixtures in our fake family.

GAUD AND BAUBLE

For big-ticket items, my mom's clients often came to the house with their husbands. Our living room became a European salon. She had a talent for charming the men as she snapped open her suitcase of shine and sparkle.

STONES

My mother specialized in semiprecious stones. Once I was standing on the stairs while she talked to a customer. I tossed a little bomb. "Hey, Mom, maybe she wants a ruby."

My mother didn't bat an eyelash. "That's precious, honey," she said. "The price is too high."

COMPETITION ON THE NORTH SHORE

Irma of Goodies' main competition for discount jewelry, Debbie Klarfeld, had a physical store in Skokie. This gave her an advantage. Customers could see all the merch. But she also had overhead—my mother could cut her on the price. Debbie promised she could get you anything. My mother promised she could get you anything cheaper. The two of them specialized in designer knockoffs and graduated from semiprecious jewelry to fine jewelry. They believed in status. They were fashion forward.

A TINY MATTER OF PERSONAL TASTE

I had a near-allergic reaction to my mother's business. I have never worn jewelry.

HAIR DYE

My mom dyed her hair in the bathroom sink. The whole bowl turned black. She had black smudges on her forehead. Once her hair turned purple. She had to call the number on the Clairol box. They told her to wash her hair.

CAR PARK

My mother had high octane. Every now and then she collapsed and stayed in bed all day. She treated herself like a car and parked in her bedroom. She called it *refueling*.

AFTER SCHOOL

My mother told people it was important for a woman to be there when her kids got home from school. She didn't think it was necessary to follow this advice.

––––––––

ON THE PHONE

My mother waltzed in around 5:15 every night. She liked to yuck it up with her friends on the phone. We could tell who she was speaking to because she sounded exactly like them.

"Hey, Mom," I shouted out, "say hi to Aunt Edie for me." She was my favorite fake aunt.

Aunt Phyllis called every night on the dot at 6:00. She was like the philosopher Kant—her routine never wavered. You could set your watch to it.

We were always in the middle of dinner. My mom said, "Hi, Phyl, I'll call you back. We're eating." Then she handed the phone to Lenie to hang up.

WHAT'S FOR DINNER?

My mom never left enough time to make dinner. She neglected to defrost the vegetables. They were still half-frozen. The meat was undercooked. Jell-O didn't have time to jell. We drank it for dessert. Once she combined a package of vanilla pudding with a package of strawberry gelatin—that was not drinkable.

My father raged about the food. We thought it was funny and bounced stuff up and down on the table. My mom could have been a consultant for Goodyear Tires. Her meals were rubbery.

Dinner was a time of great hilarity. Things changed later. After Lenie and I went to college, my mom became a good cook. The family quieted down.

CHICKEN, BLOODY CHICKEN

My mom served bloody chicken. My dad complained that chicken should be "falling off the bone." My mom turned to us for a neutral point of view. We nodded appreciatively. We said the chicken was delicious. Later, we all agreed that rare chicken is disgusting.

CELEBRATORY DINNER

Whenever I got laryngitis, my mom served steak to celebrate the fact that I couldn't talk. That was tough to swallow.

CARROTS

My dad hated carrots. He started yelling every time my mother made them. Years later we asked her why she continued to serve them when she knew she would get such a violent reaction. She was surprised. "Oh," she said, "I didn't know he didn't like carrots."

SMOKED OYSTERS

There were two cans of Reese's smoked oysters that nestled in the back of the cabinet for twenty-five years.

THE GROCERY LIST

"There's a bottle of ketchup in the cabinet," my mom said. I looked; it wasn't there. She turned to my dad. "Kurt, put that on the list!" Good one. There was no list.

TEN TIPS FROM IRMA HIRSCH, NUTRITIONIST

Avoid fresh fruit. It is filled with sugar.
Fruit cocktail is a healthy substitute, especially with Cool Whip.
Canned peaches are good in summer.
Vegetables should be canned or frozen.
Don't eat anything that looks like it comes from the ground.

Iceberg lettuce is okay in moderation.

Too much salad is unhealthy.

Margarine is better than butter.

Don't drink water. It makes you gain weight.

If you don't eat chocolate, you will never gain weight.

MELON BALLS

My mother mocked my father for bringing home fresh peaches and plums. She loathed fruit. Melon balls were the exception. Nothing says elegance like baskets of watermelon, cantaloupe, and honeydew melon balls adorning the table. Lenie spent hours scooping them out. My mother was irritated when guests ate them.

FREEZER WARS

Battle lines were drawn. You could tell who was sneaking the Neapolitan ice cream, who was allied with whom as layers disappeared. My mother ate the chocolate, Nancy and my dad ate the strawberry, Lenie and I favored the vanilla.

A slab of strawberry ice milk was left over in the freezer so long it formed red icicles.

Your friends noticed the metallic taste of vanilla pound cake stored in aluminum foil.

Nancy just wanted a taste. She took a bite out of every donut.

The box of green peas was covered in white mist.

The ice cubes looked like they had been left out in the rain.

You could see my mother's fingerprints on the snowballs she rolled in coconut for company.

SANDWICH LESSONS

My dad complained that we ate all the food in the house. Then he started buying stuff that no one else would eat.

Light on meat and heavy on bread, my dad's heroes were anemic.

Spam is salty and lives forever.

The head cheese was headed for the hero. It was slimy and slipped out of the sandwich. I half expected it to crawl across the countertop and swallow my hand.

My dad's liver sausage was no worse than his liverwurst. They were equally bad.

My dad complained because he could not make a chicken salad sandwich as great as the one at the hospital cafeteria.

It was best to avoid the kitchen on Saturday afternoon. My dad loved summer sausage, cotto salami, and Limburger cheese.

THE CRUMB-FEST

My dad dropped by the Salerno Cookie Factory on Division Street and came home with brown paper bags filled with broken butter cookies. We couldn't ring the cookies around our fingers. There were always crumbs scattered in the cabinets. We called it "the crumb-fest." Ants were invited. They came.

TIME FOR LUNCH

We were not allowed to buy lunch at school. It cost thirty-five cents. We were the outcasts who brought lunch from home. My mother gave us stale peanut butter sandwiches in a paper bag. She never added jelly. She wrapped the sandwiches in wax paper. The wax paper unwrapped. It always seemed like we were eating the ends of the bread. She added broken butter cookies. For years I tossed the sandwich, grabbed the cookies, and headed out to the playground for recess. But one day a teacher noticed what I was doing and called home. After that, I had to sit at the lunch table and gag.

TIME FOR A TV DINNER

We set trays in front of the black-and-white television set in the rec room. I don't recall eating the TV dinners. Maybe that was the point. The food was so bland you forgot it and paid attention to the show.

AFTER DINNER

My dad went rogue and walked across the park to the Jewel Supermarket on Touhy Avenue. He bought a pint of peach ice cream. He ate it himself in front of the television set. No one said anything. You didn't mess with the man when he was in that kind of mood.

SIDEKICK

Nancy was my dad's sidekick. Sometimes he took her with him to the Jewel. He bought her a chocolate bar. They palled around on Saturdays. My dad was a politic father. He tried to treat everyone equally. But he couldn't help himself. He beamed when Nancy entered the room. Lenie and I were plebes. Nancy had rank.

17

MY FATHER'S GRIEF

The only time I ever saw my dad cry was at his mother's funeral. Two tears ran down the side of one eye.

?

My fifth-grade teacher Mr. Vaughn called on me before I raised my hand. My face scrunched up like a question mark. I was always looking for an answer.

WHAT ARE YOU?

Mr. Vaughn posed a question to the class. "Are you an animal, a vegetable, or a mineral?" Everyone said "Animal" but Roger, who was a vegetarian. He said "Vegetable."

A STRONGMAN

I was a strongman for Halloween. My dad rigged up a broom with boxes on either end. Each one said "600 lbs." That was my power bar. I used it to demonstrate the deadlift. It brought in extra loot when we were trick-or-treating because no one wanted to see the trick.

HOUSE TO AVOID

The rabbi was always home. He hated Halloween. "It's not our holiday!" he shouted and slammed the door in your face.

INAUGURATION DAY, 1961

My family watched Robert Frost reciting a poem at John F. Kennedy's inauguration. He couldn't see the page in the sunlight and seemed befuddled. He recovered and recited "The Gift Outright" from memory. I didn't know how to take the gift. It was a moment of dignity that I missed.

INAUGURATION NIGHT

Ask not what your birthday party can do for you, ask what you can do for your birthday party.

WINTER GAMES

God gave us the Sabbath for rest. He gave us a snow day for fun. He gave us the hill. We provided the toboggans. He gave us ice. We supplied the skates. He tossed down snow. We made a snowman. Our poor guy was thin. He had a stony smile, but his eyes were Life Savers.

LET'S PLAY BALL

I studied the backs of baseball cards. That's how I knew that I have the same birthday as Gene Stephens. It would be neat to bat lefthanded and play left field for the Boston Red Sox.

I also have the same birthday as Camilo Pascual. It would be even neater to come from La Habana and pitch for the Minnesota Twins.

I loved it when my dad took me to Wrigley Field on a weekday in April. It cost sixty cents for a bleacher seat. We sat in the sun and shouted to the outfielders. We were bleacher bums!

This holy ground used to be a seminary.

The grass is greener than the stuff on TV. Where do they show the commercials between innings?

"This is forever, Dad." Stan the Man hit a homer over my head and Walt Moryn made an obscene gesture to the fans.

Wrigley Field is nicknamed "the Friendly Confines," but it was not friendly when two guys started a fistfight over a foul ball. They were good hitters, but they got hauled out in cuffs.

"Get off it!" my friend Donny shouted. "You went to a double-header and the Cubs lost both games." I had a stomachache from three hotdogs and a sunburn to prove it.

You had to choose between the Cubs and the White Sox. I grew up on the North Side. That made me a Cubs fan. I had a secret crush on the White Sox infield duo of Luis Aparicio and Nellie Fox, but I never confessed. Instead, I rooted for their American League rivals, the New York Yankees. This equaled out because the Cubs always lost, and the Yankees always won.

I changed my loyalty when my dad took us to a night game at Comiskey Park. Then I rooted for the South Siders.

On the playground, the argument got heated over who was the better shortstop, Banks or Aparicio. Everyone called Ernie Banks "Mr. Cub." No one called Luis Aparicio "Mr. White Sox." That was reserved for Minnie Miñoso, "the Cuban Comet." We agreed he was the best left fielder. Or was he? What about Billy Williams?

The Sox had Sherm Lollar behind the plate. He was an All Star. The Cubs had Dick Bertell. He was not an All Star, but he came from Oak Park, like Ernest Hemingway.

I used a piece of chalk to outline a batter's box on the school wall. Then I fired a pink rubber ball past imaginary hitters. They went down whiffing. I was untouchable.

I switched it up and smashed the Spaldeen out of the park. I was alone, and so there was no one to catch it. I trotted around the bases while the stands went wild.

My favorite book? *Fear Strikes Out.* My favorite moment? Jimmy Piersall took out a squirt gun and shot water on the plate so the umpire could see it better.

I was trying to grow my baseball-card collection but didn't have the cash. My mom wouldn't let me buy packs. I was good at lagging, and my cousin Mickey had a lot more cards than I did. I couldn't help myself—one Sunday afternoon, I took him to the cleaners.

Work it in like a grapefruit. A sixteen-inch softball softens so you can play it with your bare hands. It is supposed to be pitched slowly. Why did the rest of the country get the game so wrong?

Paul Brown lived a block away from Fairview School. He had a limp and a golden retriever named Tawny. He pitched for both teams in our pickup softball games. He had a good arc and topspin on his underhand pitch. We went over to his house for snacks after school. No one knew anything about him or why he was so lonely.

MARBLES

We set up the marbles in a ring and knuckled down. This was a serious game. No quitsies, keepsies. Elephant stomping was allowed. I favored a cat's-eye, Donny liked a beachball. You could use a boulder to score a peewee. We rolled until someone stopped the game in tears. The losses were too momentous. We were upset and changed the rules. Quitsies, no keepsies. Elephant stomping was not allowed.

LET'S GO FISHING

My dad took us fishing. We got up at 5 a.m. The light was cloudy. We parked by the lake and scrambled over the rocks. But then we sat there dangling our feet off the pier. I tangled my line. I was allergic to minnows. When I reeled in a fish, I couldn't touch it.

THE SUN ALSO RISES

The sun rises over Lake Michigan. It also rises elsewhere, too, but you could have fooled me. The sun sets somewhere over Oak Park.

MOM AND ME

Lenie invented a game for Nancy and her. "I'll be Mom," Lenie said, "and you be me." Nancy thought it would be fun to play.

"Okay, Lenie," Lenie said, "get me a glass of water." Nancy fetched the water.

"Okay, Lenie, hang up my dress." Nancy got the hanger.

"Hey, Lenie, your mother needs a snack." Nancy came back with cookies.

"Okay, Lenie," Lenie said finally, "make my bed."

Nancy said, "But you're still sitting in the bed."

Lenie said, "So." Nancy made the bed with Lenie in it. "Now give me a kiss," Mom said. Nancy dutifully pecked her on the cheek.

Lenie loved this game and wanted to play it every week. Nancy wasn't enthusiastic. It was no fun being Lenie. Lenie agreed. She didn't like the role either.

A CUB SCOUT, A BLUEBIRD, AND A BROWNIE

My mom signed me up to be a Cub Scout. She was the scout leader. On the first night, she sent me to my room for misbehavior. I thought this was unfair and quit. My mom resigned too. I never earned a badge.

My mom signed Lenie up to be a Bluebird. She wanted her to be a Camp Fire Girl. Lenie lasted a week. She never made it to the part about camping out.

Nancy was a Brownie for one meeting.

ON NOT BECOMING A BOY SCOUT

I thought the Boy Scouts were goody-two-shoes and never joined. But I wish I had learned to tie a knot or start a fire. In our family, survival skills would have come in handy.

————

ON POINT AT POINT GUARD

Coach Strongin showed me how to dribble with either hand. He taught me to move my feet on defense. He convinced me to shovel the court on the playground so I could play outside when it snowed. He promoted me to the junior-high team. I was his new point guard on the Fairview Falcons! It was like being called up to the Bulls.

The Fairview fans were not using their noggins when they put on those green-and-white beanies.

Our gym doubled as a theater. I crashed into an elevated stage diving for a loose ball. Coach raced to help me up. I stepped back onto the court. The show must go on.

ROLE OF A LIFETIME

This was the stage where Lenie made her acting debut as the Statue of Liberty. She was sturdy and stood there with her arm raised in the air. She welcomed a boy and a girl to Ellis Island. She said, "Greetings, tired children." This was also her farewell role.

FASHION SHOW

Lenie had to sew a dress for home economics. She couldn't manage the sleeves and had the cheapest cloth. Her dress was so poorly made that the teacher made her the announcer at the fashion show. There was a makeshift runway in the gym. Lenie used her most booming voice. She made it sound like Christian Dior debuting "the New Look."

NOT CHEERING

Lenie tried out as a cheerleader. She didn't make the team. Our mom was so enraged she called the coach. The explanation baffled her. Lenie had athletic skills, but she wouldn't cheer. She refused to jump up and down and shout *rah-rah sis-boom-bah*.

GYM CLASS

The gym teacher blew a whistle. Everyone ran for a scooter. It was a free-for-all for forty-five minutes on the gym floor. You flailed about and crashed into each other. Then the teacher blew a whistle again. Everyone lined up and politely stacked the scooters in a closet.

I did fifteen push-ups and two hundred sit-ups. My arms hurt.

The rope was hooked to the ceiling of the gym. Everyone's strength has a ceiling. Mine was close to the floor.

My two somersaults did not count as floor exercise.

I grabbed the rings and tried to muscle up, but the rings had more muscle. They were steady and still. I was not.

I stood between the parallel bars. I could get up, but I was not a swinger.

I kept my chin up, but I couldn't do one.

I was a cowboy who kept falling off his horse.

HOME SCHOOLING

My mom decided it was time to expand our vocabulary. She got out the family dictionary. She started on the letter A. The lesson lasted five minutes. The only word we learned from her was *abhor*.

Lenie and I worked the word into a routine. "That's abhorrent!" I shouted. "I abhor you for using such an abhorrent word," she replied. We thought the game was funny. My mom hated it.

THREE TEACHERS

1.

The shop teacher Mr. Gross earned his name.

2.

We were trying to irritate the substitute. We were not trying to reduce her to tears. It was puzzling when she ran out of the room.

3.

The music teacher Mr. Meyers asked me if I had a tin ear. I said, "Like a tin bell?" He said, "Just mouth the words."

NICKNAMES

"I wonder why we never use nicknames," Belly said.

SICK DAY

When I wanted to skip school, I got up at 5:30 to make frequent trips to the bathroom. My parents started to hear the toilet flush at regular intervals. They realized I had diarrhea. School was out of the question. The only flaw with my plan was that my mom overdid Phillips' Milk of Magnesia. I was constipated for days.

The bland diet for an upset stomach was nicknamed BRAT: bananas, rice, applesauce, toast. But in our house, the bananas were always rotten. I had to eat RAT.

I woke up with a tremendous stomachache. I thought I was having an appendix attack. My parents rushed me to the emergency room. The doctor diagnosed me: severe constipation. Treatment: an enema.

My mother gave us a geography lesson. She said a head cold came down from Canada. Diarrhea and constipation came up from Florida.

The trouble with school was that you didn't get to read much. When I stayed home, I could go through all four seasons of the Bronc Burnett sport books. I told a teacher that I liked *The Three-Two Pitch* and *Rough Stuff*. She predicted that I would love *Crime and Punishment* and *War and Peace*. She was right.

CHORES

We never had regular chores around the house. But my mother did not like it when Lenie and I read too much—she thought it was bad for our eyes. This motivated her to assign us tasks. She'd find us reading and suddenly, the lawn needed mowing, or the laundry had to be folded. We had to hop to it. After that, she forgot about it for another couple of weeks until she saw us curled up on our beds with a book.

THE COST OF ELECTRICITY

My dad was so obsessed with the cost of electricity that he turned off the lights whenever we left our rooms. I went to the bathroom. When I came back, the light was off.

Sometimes he turned off the lights when we were still in our rooms. He said to me, "You really don't need this reading light." I was reading.

There was also a battle over the thermostat. The reptile kept it cold. My mom and I turned it back up when he wasn't looking. But he had good night vision and turned it down again. We shivered and retaliated.

COMIC BOOKS

We were not allowed to buy comics. My mom thought they were a waste of money. If one did happen to find its way into the house, you kept it under your pillow and read it with a flashlight at night. You hid it behind the encyclopedia in the bookcase. You smuggled it out in the morning and traded it.

PETTY CRIME

My friend Scooter had fast hands. He could pocket a candy bar in a flash. He lifted all kinds of stuff—combs, key chains, bubble gum, canned sodas. Sometimes he chanced a ring or a necklace, but that was dangerous. He worked on commission, too. He could get you the right comic book for a price.

LITERARY CORRECTION

At an MLA convention in Chicago, I read a poem about a science project that I had constructed for Parents' Day, 1962. I had used wire hangers and rubber balls to illustrate the motion of planetary bodies. My mother piped up from the back row: "That's not how I remember it. Your father made that project for you."

IN THE CLASSROOM

I had only one class that was truly valuable for my future: typing. It was taught by the principal's secretary.

|| 18 ||

FIRST CRUSHES

I had a crush on Miss Cheesecake and looked for her whenever my grandmother took me to Davidson's Bakery. They gave me a kichel, which was like swallowing sweet air, but my fantasy was never around. I had to settle for seeing her in ads.

I sat behind Peggy in sixth grade. All day I tried not to pull her ponytail. I was proud of my self-control. She told everyone that I didn't like her.

You looked forward to Red Rover at recess. The girl you liked was on the other side. You were both for her and against her. "Red Rover, Red Rover, let Rosie come over!"

Dodgeball in gym class. You were evading colorful balls left and right. They were shooting at you from all directions. The girl you liked threw one wildly. She taunted you into trying to catch it.

Kickball in gym class. When she aimed at your head, you knew she liked you.

The ruling came down from the front office. No more tackle football games between boys and girls on the front lawn.

Flag football was still allowed. We found ways to de-flag each other.

CHANGING MORES AT THE SCHOOL DANCE

At the first school dance, we stood up straight and kept our hands at our sides.

At the second school dance, we slouched and started to twist.

At the third school dance, we flapped our arms and clicked our heels for the mashed potato.

COURTLY LOVE, ELEMENTARY SCHOOL EDITION

I crashed my red J. C. Higgins bicycle on Barbara's lawn after school. She stood in the bay window and waved while I dusted off the dirt.

Every day she wore a different-colored blouse. I liked it when she shook out her ponytail or put on a baseball cap. Once she passed me a note on the windowsill: "Don't come tomorrow. My father will be home early."

"Eddie and Barbie sitting in a tree / K-I-S-S-I-N-G."

The tree was the top of a monkey bar set in a small, out-of-the-way park near the expressway. No one used this park. It was simply there. We had discovered the power of the secret getaway.

"First comes love, then comes marriage, / Then comes baby in a baby carriage."

—————

SEVENTH GRADE

Fairview South was one long building. You walked down an extended hallway into junior high school and puberty.

DREAM GIRL

I dreamt about Marla. I woke up with something sticky in my pajamas. I was too self-conscious to ask about it.

SLUMBER PARTIES

Lenie's slumber parties were off-limits. I was confined to quarters. But I could sit in the closet and hear the conversation. There was talk about boys. Sometimes my name came up and Lenie said, "Ooogh, gross." I got excited by the pillow fights.

WATER BOMBS

My dad went ballistic when Lenie started playing with the water balloons that she found in the drawer next to his bed. She tore them out of packages. We called them *water bombs*.

My mom went ballistic when she found extra-heavy water bombs in the glove compartment of my dad's car.

THE TIMER

At the make-out party, there was a pimply faced referee timing everyone with a stopwatch.

AMUSEMENT PARK

The Tilt-A-Whirl was bad enough. You did not want to be stuck with the wrong person floating through the interminable Tunnel of Love.

TO A TWELVE-YEAR-OLD BOY GETTING ON
A FERRIS WHEEL WITH A GIRL

If you get queasy when the cage rocks and lurches into the air, stay on the ground.

MY GREASER GIRLFRIEND

Chris was cool. She had short blond hair and wore a black leather jacket. One day she handed me a Camel in the alley behind her house. I coughed so hard that I never smoked again.

Chris was tough. I didn't care if she got in fights so long as she didn't fight with me. I didn't care whom she talked about as long as she talked about them with me.

Chris was faster than I was. She said I was slow for someone smart.

Chris said it was a contest for ultimate redness between my tight red pants and my shiny red bike. My face won.

I looked sunny wearing yellow pants.

Cool to guide Chris to a corner booth for fries and a cherry Coke at Jake's. Uncool to pay with coins.

Chris was a year older than I was. This did not matter when we were in junior high. It was a different story when she entered high school. I was riding my bicycle when I spotted her on a motorcycle with a guy in a bomber jacket.

Chris's father was a policeman. Just after I started driving, he pulled me over for running a stop sign. "You ran a lot of those with my daughter," he said, and let me off with a warning.

The Skokie Theatre was founded in 1912 so Chris and I could make out in the back row fifty years later. It once showed silent movies that were shot nearby. Now we were silent, but the movies were singing. Our favorite was *Bye Bye Birdie.* Conrad Birdie twitched his hips on the flickering screen and the girls screamed in the dark.

Years later I published a poem called "The Skokie Theatre." I mentioned that Chris had touched me below the belt. "What happens if she reads that poem?" my mother asked. "She'll be embarrassed." I told her this seemed unlikely because Chris left school early. My mother said, "There's always continuing education."

TEMPER, TEMPER

My dad had chronic bouts of anger, but otherwise never got sick.

My parents didn't have a punishment policy. They just lost their tempers. If I mouthed off, my dad went nuts. I had to sprint for my room when he lost it. While he was chasing me down in my closet, my mother charged behind him calling out, "Not in the face, not in the face!"

Rules of the house: It is open season for boys, but girls do not get hit.

When my mom got mad, she threw a hairbrush at me and missed. She had poor aim.

Once she hit me with a cheap broom. The bristles came off in my hands.

My mom wasn't winning the argument. She shouted, "Kurt, the kids are disrespecting me!"

My dad didn't like being bothered. He came out yelling, "Don't disrespect your mother!" He didn't know what he was yelling about. I didn't hang around to find out.

When my mom said my dad was "complex," she was rationalizing something he had done, which she had instigated.

CLOCKED

I got mad when Howie butted in front of me at Little League tryouts. He challenged me to a fight. I accepted. He led me to a grove of trees.

"Are you ready?" he asked. I nodded.

Howie clocked me with one punch. I got up. He knocked me down again. I was bleeding badly. I kept standing up and getting knocked down until one of the coaches came over and broke it up.

THE LITTLE GUY

I was tall and skinny. Howie was short and stocky. He was tough and knew how to fight. I didn't have a clue. My dad chortled when he heard about it. He couldn't help himself. He always rooted for the little guy.

KURT'S FAVORITE FIGHTER

Dov-Ber "Beryl" Rosofsky grew up on Maxwell Street. He had small hands, brittle bones, and a father who was a rabbi. This was Barney Ross, who wore a blue-and-white terrycloth bathrobe that said, "The Pride of the Ghetto." Kurt talked about the night in 1933 that Ross beat Tony Canzoneri to become the lightweight and junior welterweight champion of the world.

MILLER AND HIS BOYS

Davey Miller sponsored Barney Ross. Kurt didn't go for mobsters, but he made an exception for Miller, one of Capone's guys, who ran a gym on Roosevelt Road. He was a bigtime boxing ref too. My dad wasn't the only one who nicknamed him "the Judah Maccabee of the West Side" because his gang beat up toughs who beat up Jews anywhere in the city, especially in Lawndale, the "Chicago Jerusalem." It was a public service. "They had our backs," Kurt said, and that was that.

THE KING

Kurt also liked Harris Krakow, who grew up with Dov-Ber Rosofsky, and came from a family of fishmongers on Maxwell Street. This was Kingfish Levinsky, the Windy City Assassin, who was kayoed by Max Baer and crushed by Joe Louis.

The King was managed by his sister Leaping Lena. He was a buffoon in the ring, and a bit of a windbag. He never jabbed with his left hand, but Kurt liked him because he used his right to punch his way out of the ghetto.

ALLIES

Kurt listened to the blow-by-blow the night that Max Baer, who wore a Star of David on his trunks, defeated Max Schmeling, Hitler's favorite fighter, at Yankee Stadium. It was a win for the Allies and won him Greta Garbo.

GOLDEN GLOVES

My dad took Lenie and me to the amateur fights. We only went once. It was more amateur than we anticipated. Some of the boxers were unprepared. They got pummeled in the first round. It was so sickening that we got sick in the stands.

BOXING LESSONS

My dad chalked out a boxing ring in the backyard. He laced up my new red gloves. I pranced around. He taught me to keep my fists up, to lean in and lean back, to jab with my left and cross with my right. Once I punched him a little too hard in the chest. He looked as if he was going to retaliate. Then he recovered and told me it was a clean hit.

———

DAMSELS IN DISTRESS

Lenie's friend Laura liked to pretend they were damsels in distress waiting to be rescued by the heroes of *Bonanza*. While Laura was fixated on being rescued by Little Joe, Lenie set her heart on Hoss.

"This game is stupid," Lenie said. "What's the point of waiting for two fake cowboys who don't even know we exist?"

"Keep your voice down," Laura said. "The kidnappers will hear you."

Laura wouldn't budge from the bed and so Lenie finally ditched her and went outside to play baseball with the boys. But Laura had refused to untie her. Lenie had to hop to the front door because her hands and feet were bound with imaginary rope.

NEWFOUND SKILL

I used my newfound skill as a boxer and broke my best friend Craig's front tooth because he did not want to let Lenie play in a pickup game. He never spoke to me again. I shouldn't have done it. But Lenie was a better ball player.

KURT HIRSCH'S FIGHT AGAINST GENDER DISCRIMINATION IN LITTLE LEAGUE BASEBALL, 1962

My dad was insistent. Lenie deserved a tryout. The men gathered on the mound with the rule book. She was a southpaw throwing bullets. She threw strike after strike. The men agreed my sister was good enough to pitch. The ball smacked in the catcher's glove. The rules stated she could not.

LITERARY CORRECTIONS

Years later I wrote a poem called "Siblings." It described Lenie's Little League tryout. I included it in a book that won a prize for Chicago literature. I sent Lenie to collect the award. She said, "I need to correct my brother. He exaggerates. I never had three pitches."

Everyone clucked. The judge said, "Poetic license."

I also talked about the rivalry between my dad and his younger brother. I set it on the golf course. My Uncle Harry didn't care about the competition. He said, "I never played golf."

WHAT BOYS DON'T LIKE

"You should always let boys win," my mother told my sister. "Boys don't like girls who are better at sports than them. They don't like girls who are smarter than them, either." My poor sister was out of luck—she was better at sports and smarter than the boys in her class.

DISTRICT CHAMPS

The regular season ended. My parents forgot about the Little League World Series. They planned a summer vacation to Washington DC. I was so miserable on the trip that they let me fly home for the district finals. This was my first flight. I sat by the window and surveyed the world. Uncle Bob met me at the airport. We played a night game under the lights at Thillens Stadium. I started behind the plate. I got the winning hit in the last inning. We won 4–3.

REGIONAL LOSERS

I was the starting catcher. Period. For the sake of fairness, the parent coach put the second-string catcher behind the plate for the next game. This was loser thinking. I pouted on the bench. I pinch-hit and was hit by a pitch. We lost at regionals. My Little League career was done for.

"TOWN WITHOUT PITY"

This was the year Lenie played Gene Pitney's "Town Without Pity" one thousand times on the record player next to her bed. It was her anthem. Nancy was only five years old. It was not her anthem. She was hoping for something more merciful.

19

SUNDAY SCHOOL

My mother loved the grandeur and pompousness of Temple Sholom on Lake Shore Drive so much that Lenie and I had to take a two-hour bus ride to Sunday school.

When our mom came to wake us up, we pretended to be asleep. It didn't work. She sat on the bed and talked until we got up.

We were picked up first at 8 a.m. When we arrived, I walked straight through the hallway and slipped out the back door. I looped around to the lake or hung out reading in a grocery store.

We were dropped off last at 2 p.m. On the busride home my sister caught me up on the lesson. It was like reading Hebrew. I learned everything backwards.

HIGH HOLIDAYS

We joined Temple Sholom so we could appear with rich people on the High Holidays. My father held the tickets. My mother stood at the top of the stairs in her mink coat. She wore her mink to schul even when the weather was warm. Impact was important. She had to sacrifice and sweat it out.

ON HIGH

My dad's cousin was a family doctor in Hyde Park. Dr. Josephin was an intellectual. My dad said he spoke perfect High German at home. But he was seldom home.

His wife, Irene, was elegant and put on airs. She liked the finer things. She was seldom home either.

They raised two well-adjusted children. Or maybe Shirley and Lester just raised themselves.

The family lived in a high rise by the lake. We visited every few years. Irene served tea and looked down on us. Dr. Josephin left to talk to a patient. He didn't look at us at all.

HOW TO MAKE SCHMALTZ AND GRIBENES

My grandmother's holiday recipe was hardcore. "Sauté the chicken skin and collect the liquid fat. Add onion and take a year off your life." She could also sew a kishke and gefilte a fish.

PASSOVER SEDER

When I chanted "Let my people go," I meant the kids.

The service was short, but it seemed long. Everyone had a different prayer book, and my dad didn't know what he was doing.

We went around the table mangling the Hebrew one by one. No one could sing the prayers in tune.

My grandmother's sides were delicious, but my mom undercooked the brisket all on her own.

It's a four-glasses-of-grape-juice kind of night.

At the end of the meal, I was the son who said it wasn't worth it to search for the afikomen. My dad hid it in the basement, and all you got was a buck for your trouble.

It was different in the Allweiss household. Elijah might want to visit their place. Uncle Morris ran a tight service, Aunt Mathilda made chocolate macaroons, and those kids got real stuff, like bicycles.

THE HEBREW ALPHABET

My mother ripped the Hebrew-letter pages from one of my grandfather's art books. She arranged them into a collage that hung in our basement. Someone noticed that the letters were out of sequence.

THE GUEST ROOM

1.

I lay under a picture of Jesus Christ in the guest room at Curt's house. Jesus looked radiantly happy, as if he'd just seen the light. I stayed awake most of the night. I was scared that he would convert me during my sleep.

2.

In the middle of the night, I took down the picture and hid it in the closet behind a suitcase. After that, I slept fine.

3.

"I must be losing my mind," Mrs. Luscombe said. She was getting the room ready. "I have no memory of taking down that picture and putting it in the closet."

THE VELVET RABBI

My mother had a painting on velvet of a wise old rabbi. It hung in her bedroom. She could counter Christian kitsch with Jewish kitsch.

The rabbi kept an eye on her. Personally, I would not have wanted him to see what I was doing in bed.

CONTRACT DISPUTE

Rabbi Binstock could find you anywhere in the house. He had a glass eye that made it seem like he was always staring at you.

Before my bar mitzvah, Rabbi Binstock glared at me until I signed a contract stating I would attend Sunday school until I was confirmed at fifteen. This was called "expanding the religious school curriculum." It was extortion.

I showed the document to Layf's father. As my lawyer, he said that the contract was non-binding because I was a minor.

I informed the rabbi the contract was invalid. My parents made me honor it anyway.

DISCOUNTED

My parents bought my dress shoes on sale at Wolinsky & Levy. There was a stamp on the sole that said DAMAGED. That's why I walked with my feet close to the ground.

"MY FAMILY"

Lenie won the sixth-grade poetry contest for her poem "My Family." This was a first. She was the official family laureate.

The poem began: "We live in a world of our own / And to others a world unknown." This was truer than anyone realized.

"My Family" put the family in a good light. My mom loved this propaganda so much she memorized it. She forced Lenie to recite it at my bar mitzvah.

Lenie did it dutifully. Her dress was pink, but her face was red for her only poetry reading.

———

HEBREW LESSON

My Hebrew name, *Elimelech*, means "God is king." My family thought it was royal. It took me twenty-five years to discover it is not. When I mentioned it to the folklorist Dan Ben-Amos, he burst out laughing. "In Israel, it's a shtetl name," he explained. "You might as well call yourself *Schlemiel*."

BAR MITZVAH

I became a man on 24 Tevet 5723.

It took a year to prepare. I was furious because I had to miss basketball practice for afterschool lessons. Traffic was snarled. How do you say "fast break" in Hebrew?

I practiced my Torah part with Lenie. The old girl knew Hebrew better than the new man.

Exodus: 1:1–6:1. My Torah reading described the enslavement of the Israelites in Egypt.

For my bar mitzvah speech, I compared life to a baseball game. Your grandparents help you get to first. Your parents help you get to second. Your teachers help you get to third. God helps you come home. My mother made me change the order. She put herself on third base.

The party was in the French Room at the Drake Hotel. My mom liked the silky décor. I liked the view of Oak Street Beach. But grown-ups kept getting in the way.

Aunt Celia came with her three children: the ghost, the mogul, and the beauty. This was the only time we met Larry. He seemed like a regular guy. "This mental illness thing is hokum," my grandmother said. "Nervous people have nerves." I was only partly paying attention. Sherwood poured me a glass of wine. I was a man now in the eyes of God. I could drink. It was okay to marry Rossie.

I was talking to a girl when Uncle Snooky wandered over to say that he used to change my diapers. She said, "How long ago was that?"

My parents got a deal from our next-door neighbor on the cake. Alex was a baker at the Palmer House. He carried it in a basket to the Drake. On a table in the center of the room, it teetered slightly off balance. The writing looked shaky. *Mitzvah* was misspelled.

Alex gave me three striped shirts from Marshall Field's. They were too small for me. When I went to exchange them, I discovered he had bought them on sale. I could only return them to him. They fit him perfectly.

What was I supposed to do with so many fountain pens? It's not like I was going to become a writer.

My parents pocketed the bonds. They gave them to me when I graduated from college.

My dad studied the bill. He immediately declared, "No more bar mitzvahs." This made my mom laugh. "You don't have any more sons," she said.

My dad regrouped. He declared, "No bat mitzvahs. I don't believe in them." This did not make my mom laugh. Or my sisters either. We all knew what he didn't believe in.

ZONE IMPROVEMENT PLAN

I became a man just before the US implemented the five-digit zip code. Ours was 60077. We all improved then.

GRAND DUCHESS

My dad wanted to see HRH *Grand Duchess Charlotte* when she came to the Luxembourg Gardens in Morton Grove. My mom said, "There's not room for two of us."

BAD LUCK ON SUNDAY MORNING

Rabbi Binstock was a Reformer. It was my bad luck that he replaced Friday-night services with Sunday-morning worship. Suddenly, there were a lot of grownups around. I had to be careful skipping out.

The good news was that he gave up the aliyot, so you couldn't get summoned to the bimah. No one noticed I was missing.

The next rabbi reformed the reformer and reinstated Friday night services. By then I had said shalom to Temple Sholom. It's convenient to have one word that means both hello and goodbye.

BOOK OF LEVITICUS

God likes a sacrificial lamb. He doesn't like a guinea pig. He wants folks who follow the rules. He doesn't put up with pishers.

"THE CONVERSION OF THE JEWS"

I read a story by Philip Roth. "I don't understand why God can do everything in the world except turn Jesus into His son," I told the rabbi. "It's as if God pitched a one-hitter."

The rabbi hit back: "God is not a pitcher."

I didn't know the rabbi detested Philip Roth. If I had known, I would have read all of Roth's stories.

A SLIGHT MISCALCULATION

"God is infallible," the rabbi said.

"Then why did He create light two days before He made the sun?"

"Because light is fixed, and the sun rotates."

This explanation didn't make sense. At least God didn't cover up His mistakes.

FAMILY HISTORY

I'm not sure what possessed me to shout out in class, "Get the Jew!"

What I got was a trip to the principal's office and a lecture from my father about the Holocaust.

That's how I found out about his relatives who died in a concentration camp. It was the only time he ever talked about them.

THE ART TEACHER

Belly and I pretended to sneeze when we said the name of the art teacher, Mr. Har*too*nian. But we knew it wasn't funny when he got called on the carpet for showing us drawings of Armenians being slaughtered by Turks. We could not unlearn what we had seen. And now we knew a new word: *genocide*.

————

LET'S TAKE THE KIDS TO THE MOVIES

My parents took Nancy and Lenie to see Alfred Hitchcock's film *The Birds* at the Skokie Theatre. They thought it was a kids' movie.

Nancy was an astute film critic. She was terrified. My dad rushed her to the street. My mom and Lenie stayed for the horror.

Nancy had nightmares for a year. She was frightened by birds. She did not become an ornithologist.

DEATH OF A PARAKEET

Nancy had a blue parakeet named Charlie. One day my mom left the cage door open. Charlie flew into a mirror. My mom said he was at the vet. It took Nancy a year to figure out the parakeet was not at the vet. It died attacking itself.

MR. PAGLIA AND PRESIDENT KENNEDY

My teacher Mr. Paglia died of a heart attack just before President Kennedy was shot. I confused the two deaths in my mind. Whenever someone started crying about President Kennedy, I thought about Mr. Paglia's children, and cried too.

THE VIOLINIST

My new girlfriend was a budding violinist. She practiced all the time. My parents thought she took advantage of me. I didn't see how that was true. "Right," my mother said. "That's because she plays you like a fiddle."

DANCE LESSONS

My parents were good dancers. They were light on their feet. Lenie and I were not. My dad decided to give us dance lessons in the basement.

Our first dance was the box step. My geometry was off. I took the linear approach. Lenie and I marched up and back, back and up.

We did better with the cha-cha-cha. We could count to three. We even won a dance contest at school. My dad got the trophy from one of his customers.

THE BEATLES

Everyone was gobsmacked when the Beatles played *Ed Sullivan*. We danced around the TV. The music was a language only teenagers could understand.

A POET AND A ONE-MAN BAND

Talent blossomed at the Rec Center on Friday night. It was our time. Simon and Garfunkel, I mean Belly and I, sang "The Sound of Silence" to a packed house. It was unrehearsed. The silence was so loud it sounded like a bomb.

Belly could really strum a guitar, so we gave it another shot and sang "I See the Moon" the next week. But the moon did not see us. Hello, Darkness, my old friend.

Our duo retired. The one-man band got the message. He grew up to become a lawyer.

HOW TO BEHAVE IN RESTAURANTS

My mother told us to order anything we wanted on the menu. We ordered the cheapest dishes. She offered us drinks. We declined. What about dessert? No takers.

IMPERMISSIBLE

My mother wanted to taste my burger. She reached over and snagged a piece from my plate. Then she grabbed my drink. This was a lifelong habit. I'm still waiting for her to ask permission.

THE GOLDEN OX

My parents planned a romantic supper at the Golden Ox on Clybourn Avenue. This was one of my dad's favorite German restaurants. He didn't want to pay for parking, so he dropped my mom off at the front door and searched for a spot. He couldn't find one. My mom was seated at a table in front. She ordered a *Leberkäse*. She didn't particularly like German food, but it was good. She paid the bill. My dad was still circling. He picked her up and they drove home.

ON DOUBLE DATES

My parents went on double dates. My mom arranged them. My dad shouted that all my mom's friends were stupid. "I'd say that all your friends are stupid too," she shouted back, "if you had any."

The men sat in the front seat of the car, the women in the back. The men didn't talk much. The women talked nonstop. The men walked with their arms at their sides. The women walked arm in arm. Everyone drank. The men paid the check. The women told them how much to tip.

GANGSTERS BY THE POOL

We drove to Florida for vacation. We stayed at the Fontainebleau Hotel on the strip in Miami Beach. The hotel was built to look like a movie set. We got a deal because it was offseason. If you knew how to look, you could spot Jewish gangsters by the pool. They wore three-piece suits. They never went to the ocean. The ocean was for suckers. We were not suckers. We liked the pool better too.

ON THE ROAD

My dad posed in front of a doghouse by the side of the road. He looked like a bulldog. Afterwards, he drove the wrong way on a one-way feeder and got a ticket. He took the doghouse with him.

Whenever my mom wanted to stop, she'd say, "Kurt, the kids are hungry." After that, we had to eat whether we were hungry or not.

My mother suddenly started singing. "I'm a Ramblin' Wreck from Georgia Tech and a heck of an engineer." We had no idea where she had picked up the Georgia Tech fight song. We were going on vacation with a jolly fellow who drank his whiskey clear.

EARLY BIRD SPECIAL

In Miami Beach, we ate dinner at 4 p.m. My mother wore a sun skirt, my dad put on white pants and a polo shirt. They looked surprisingly young in their summer outfits. All the other kids were there with their grandparents.

UNCLE HARRY AND AUNT MOLLY

My grandmother had two sisters and five brothers, whom she called "the kids." They were blanks to us. We only met Uncle Abe and Aunt Gussy a few times. They looked like Jimmy Durante. We did know Uncle Harry, who looked like Mr. Magoo, and Aunt Molly. They were short people who lived in a small house in a cul-de-sac in Miami. I towered over them. Whenever we visited, they served a tiny lunch.

VACATION PENS

Lenie and I ran up the Stairs to Nowhere. We had nowhere to go so we ran back down. Then we raced through the hallways stealing ballpoint pens from housekeeping carts. We used these pens to write postcards. They were vacation pens. They only wrote about Florida.

FASHION ADVICE FOR THE POOL

1.

"Dad, that's not a Speedo. You're wearing the bottom of Aunt Phyllis's bathing suit. It's too tight. Your junk is showing."

2.

"Dad, don't wear boxers under your bathing suit."

DEAD MAN'S FLOAT

My dad freaked us with his dead man's float in the swimming pool at night. It was too lifelike.

20

GO TO HULL

My mom took her share of the money from the Carroll Avenue property and bought a two-flat apartment building on Hull Street in Skokie.

Ruby bought her a building, once removed. This building was gray: physically and spiritually. This was not Hull House. No one here was settling anyone.

My mom rented the flats to people we never met. It was a phone game when the renters called. Whoever answered lost. The calls were complaints.

Lenie and I mowed the lawn and took out the trash. We helped our dad clean the basement when it flooded. It flooded all the time.

My mom never visited the place. She just said, "Go to Hull."

It sounded like she was telling us off.

TECUMSEH PARK

Lenie and I skipped over to Tecumseh Park on the corner of Hull and Terminal. Tecumseh was a Shawnee warrior and chief. After he was killed in the Battle of the Thames in 1813, American soldiers stripped and scalped his body. The tribal confederacy fell apart. It took a while for the Skokie Park District to name a playground after him. The place was peaceful, but I'm sure it did not appease Tecumseh's ancestors.

OAKTON STREET

You could walk from Hull to Oakton in downtown Skokie. It was once called Harms Avenue. It started out with a general store and still had shops.

We did not have money to shop in them. But there was a Ben Franklin five-and-dime. Old Ben was thrifty. They had stuff we could afford.

There was a new public pool. It was filled with girls in bathing suits. There was a new public library. It was filled with girls reading books.

Aunt Elaine worked her entire adult life at Levine's dress shop. Lenie and I passed there a thousand times. We never looked in.

THREE SPOTS

1.

You could gamble over a steak sandwich at Krier's Restaurant. We never won or lost because our parents were too tight to take us there.

2.

My dad took us for ice cream to Cock Robin on Skokie Blvd. The ice cream was square. The name was worse than square. It was downright embarrassing.

3.

Raymond's Work-n-Sport was located next door to the Christian Science Reading Room on Lincoln Avenue. You could shop in one place and shun the other. It was like a punch line to a Jewish joke.

THE JOKE

A Jew was stranded on a desert island. He built two synagogues. When he was rescued, they asked him why he built two houses of worship. He said, "That's the one I pray in. That's the one I wouldn't be caught dead in."

SUNDAY NIGHT

My grandmother said that Chinese American cuisine reached its pinnacle at the Canton Restaurant on Lincoln Avenue.

She loved the egg foo young. Aunt Celia could make a fluffy omelet, but she couldn't compare to the cook at Canton.

Matzo ball soup is family. Wonton soup is an adopted child. You love it just the same.

FORTUNE COOKIE

My fortune was preposterous: "Someday you will look back fondly on the past."

CRYING POOR

Our mom said that her new friend Phyllis L. was "crying poor" when she complained that she didn't have any money. Lenie and I thought it was literally true. We put our heads together and decided to give poor Phyllis a hanky and some babysitting cash for her birthday. Mom nixed the idea. Poor Mouth was rich.

WHY POOR P. L. WAS RICH

Phyllis's first husband, Marty, was a doctor. She put him through medical school and got a huge payout when he left her for a nurse.

She bleached her hair and picked up a second husband who shall remain nameless. He just lounged around and spent her dough. She considered herself lucky because he kicked the bucket before she needed to kick him out.

Phyllis's third husband, Fred, was an optometrist who invested well in the market. Everyone said he was far-sighted.

PAYING JOBS

I once asked my mom for an allowance. She looked at me as if I had asked her for one of Saturn's rings. She did not make allowances or give them.

When it came to working, Mom was eager to push us out the starting gate. It was Depression-era mentality. What difference did it make it if was 1936 or 1963?

You babysat, mowed lawns, shoveled snow, ran errands, delivered papers, painted houses. You were on someone's books, or you were off their books. It didn't matter. You got up early. You ingratiated yourself. You worked.

THE ALMIGHTY

My parents never thought we showed sufficient respect for the almighty dollar. They thought we underestimated its true power. What did they want us to do, salute?

––––––––

NEPOTISM

My Uncle Bob's parents were two of eight relatives, four siblings and their spouses, who owned Robert's Delicatessen on Devon and Western in Westridge. My mom used her pull to get Lenie and me our first jobs there. Some nepotisms pay poorly.

CLASS CONSCIOUSNESS

My sister was a waitress, I was a busboy. Waitresses speak to customers and get tips, busboys do not. Waitresses take a break at a well-lit table in the corner, busboys go to a dank room in the basement. Waitresses eat roast beef, busboys eat burgers.

PUNCH THE CLOCK

The jeweler Willard Legrand Bundy invented the time clock in 1888. I wish I could have punched him in 1964. Instead, I punched his invention every day at 8 a.m. and 4 p.m.

The timestamp meant I belonged to someone else eight hours per day. There were two fifteen-minute breaks, one half-hour for lunch. This was my freshman year in the School of Shit-Jobs.

CHEAPSKATE

My dad came in and harassed the waitress for so long a guy down the counter told him to cut it out. My dad laughed. He confessed the waitress was his daughter. He left her a five-buck tip. My sister was shocked. That was the most money the cheapskate ever gave her.

RULES OF ENGAGEMENT

My parents came into the restaurant and sat in a middle booth. They kept trying to talk to me while I was busing tables. I refused. It was unprofessional.

IN THE FREEZER

I was picking up a pan of frozen kreplach. For one eternal moment, the heavy door started to swing shut behind me. I caught it just in time. I did not freeze.

SODA FOUNTAIN JERK

I was such a mediocre busboy that I was promoted to soda fountain jerk. There was no salary hike.

The heat was on. I was situated between the grill, which sizzled, and the deli counter, which steamed.

The young guys behind the grill flirted with the waitresses, the old men behind the deli counter kibbitzed with the customers.

Move to New York if you want an egg cream. If you want it the Chicago way, I'll squirt chocolate syrup into soda water and phosphoric acid. Here's a chocolate phosphate.

Warm up in the late morning. 12:15 is game time.

It's hard to prepare for four waitresses yelling at you at the same time.

Anyone who ordered a malt was inconsiderate.

"One chocolate malt, one strawberry milkshake, one vanilla phosphate. One hot fudge sundae, extra whipped cream. Make it snappy. Oh, change that vanilla phosphate to a chocolate phosphate. Drop the strawberry shake. It should be a vanilla shake. I need it right away. Why'd you give me a chocolate malt? I said chocolate milkshake. Get on it. Change that hot fudge sundae to a banana split. . . ."

No time for moping. Mop it up.

Every day at 3 p.m., I scanned the extra drinks. I lined them up on the counter and took a deep breath to prepare myself. One by one, I gulped down my mistakes.

RETURNS

The waitress returned to waitressing, but the jerk did not come back to the soda fountain.

———

AT THE BARBECUE

I'd die of shame if I had to wear black knee-highs and white Bermuda shorts, like my dad.

Objectively speaking, my dad was bad at the barbecue. The coals were not hot, and the meat was cheap. Best to stick to hot dogs.

My grandmother's friends Muttie, Sylvia, and Ida came to our house for Independence Day. They looked patriotic in their red, white, and blue beehives.

My dad couldn't get Muttie's nickname straight. He kept calling her Muddy, like a bluesman.

My dad barbecued one last time for the season. We were relieved when he hung up his prongs.

BABYSITTING

The Sorkins had four kids. I let them tire themselves out. The key was to keep them from killing each other.

I learned the gentle raid of a cabinet. If you were careful, it looked like you didn't touch anything at all.

The Sorkins were always late; this meant that I got paid more. The car door woke me up.

At the end of the night, Mr. Sorkin went downstairs to pour a drink. Mrs. Sorkin told me to sit on the bed and talk to her.

"Don't mind me," she said and changed into a nightgown. I had never seen a woman in underwear.

Mr. Sorkin came back up.

DON'T KID A KIDDER

I told my mother that I liked talking to Mr. and Mrs. Sorkin. "Don't kid a kidder," she said. "He's sloshed and you like talking to her because she's a swinger."

REAL CHEESE

The Yedlins had the best stuff in their fridge. They had real cheese and everything. They were upset when Lenie cleaned them out during a long babysitting stint on Saturday night. They called our parents and came up with a list of what she could eat. It was no fun, and she didn't like babysitting for them anymore.

REFRIGERATOR PARENTS

Alex and Edith had a son named Mitchell. My parents thought that Mitchell was different because Alex and Edith were refrigerator parents.

This was an idea of blame popularized by Bruno Bettelheim at the University of Chicago. It meant that the parents of autistic children have no emotional warmth.

I didn't know there was such a thing as autism. But I babysat for Mitchell and observed that Alex and Edith were not cold at all. They were warm. If anything, they were oven parents. The oven was turned on high.

MIMICRY

Mitchell mimicked me with a difference. I said *Marcia*, he repeated *Marla*. I mentioned *cookies*, he responded *cooties*. I asked him if he liked *mimicking* me. He said he liked *mocking* me.

KITCHEN-TABLE TALK

Alex and I sat at the kitchen table after everyone else had gone to bed. He served me a cup of green tea. I had no idea he lived in Shanghai during the war. That's where he became a pastry chef.

The city was occupied by the Japanese, and Alex learned to make wagashi. My schlubby neighbor created desserts shaped like delicate flowers, fruits, and leaves.

You had to see it to believe it. Alex shaped wafers into cherry blossoms. He made a cake that looked like a raindrop.

BASEBALL CARDS

1.

I created my own game of fantasy baseball. My two beds, which were arranged in an L, served as a lopsided field. I created All-Star teams. The players took the field. The ball was a penny. The hitter was a card. I was busy slapping the coin, moving the fielders, and running the bases all at the same time.

Lenie heard me talking through the door. She dropped by for the color commentary.

"It's a hard grounder to the left side of the infield. Banks goes deep into the hole to backhand it, swivels around, and nabs his man with a rifle to first. He got him by half a step. Kaline is challenging the call. He better watch it, or he'll get thrown out of the game. He was clearly out. What an arm! One away."

"It wasn't as clear as all that," Lenie said. "I think he was safe."

2.

When I started high school, my mother decided I was too old to fool around with baseball cards. It took me years to put together a collection. One day she simply tossed it in the trash.

I was outraged when I came home from school. It was a mean thing to do. Later she regretted it. Not because of my feelings. But because she had thrown away thousands of dollars of merch.

CREW CUT

My mom and dad believed that a boy should have short hair. So did my coaches. As a result, the barber cut my hair so short I didn't know it was curly until I went to college.

AT THE DENTIST

The Gag was on me.

The new dental assistant was assigned to Lenie—the Gag was on her too.

I had a front tooth that bucked out of control. But after they sawed it down, my bark was worse than my overbite.

My mom took us to the cheapest dentist. He made extra money drilling good teeth.

She took me to the cheapest orthodontist too. But no one noticed I had bad braces because I didn't smile for a year.

Then I got my first crummy retainer.

GRADUATION SPEECHES

Lenie and I gave eighth-grade graduation speeches two years in a row. We talked about becoming independent adults. Our dad was proud, our mom disapproved. She said, "Too soon."

REUNION

We still act as if there is someone with an open ledger writing it all down in the principal's office after school.

21

HIGH-SCHOOLING IT

There were three Niles high schools: East, West, and North.

Niles East was founded in 1938. It was a young adult. Niles North was just opening its doors. It was a baby. Niles West was built in 1959. It was a first grader.

Some of my Fairview classmates were Easterners. A few moved North. There was no South. That would have been my favorite direction. But like a true pioneer, I went West.

We chanted, "West is best, East is least, and North is air-conditioned." The part about air-conditioning was true.

EXPRESSWAY

I was one year older than Edens Expressway. There were weeds and wildflowers spreading by the side of the road. We were fenced in.

You could see Edens from our school on Oakton Street. I gazed at it longingly. Paradise was driving away.

A BELL RANG

A bell rang to start the school day. It rang at the end of each period. The periods were like rounds in a prizefight. Each round was forty-five minutes. The fight lasted seven rounds. The bell was shrill. It served a purpose. It united people. Everyone hated high school.

HOMEROOM

Homeroom was the warm-up before a game no one wanted to play. The teacher took attendance. The loudspeaker blared announcements. No one listened. The principal had a repellent voice. Sometimes a perky student came on to perk everyone up. We percolated down. Then the bell rang for first period. Everyone rushed into the hallway. There was music. It was the sound of five hundred lockers slamming in the early morning.

HOW I BECAME A PASS RECEIVER

My mother swore at my birth that I would not play football. She forgot this solemn oath until I entered high school.

I begged and pleaded. This was unbecoming for a future football player. My mom was unmoved. I enlisted my dad. He had no luck. Then he handed the ball to my Uncle Bob, who ran over my mom's arguments.

I was five days late for tryouts. When I trotted onto the field for practice, the coach asked me what position I played. I said, "Quarterback."

"We already have a quarterback," he replied. "You'll be an end." That's how I ended up.

The coach sent me to the freshman B team. I decided to quit. My father wouldn't hear of it. "Quit whining," he said. "I'm not raising a quitter."

TWO COMMANDMENTS

I mocked the sign over the whirlpool: YOU CAN'T MAKE THE CLUB IN THE TUB. I mocked the sign over the trainer's door: WHEN YOU CALL ON A JACKASS HE KICKS, WHEN YOU CALL ON A RACEHORSE HE RUNS. But I stayed out of the whirlpool. I ran. In midseason, I got a call from on high. The overlord had smiled down. I had fulfilled the two commandments. I was promoted to the freshman A team.

THE SORROW OF MANLY SPORTS

At Niles West, I cried into my eye black every time we lost a football game. This lasted four years.

HOW TO GET SENT TO DETENTION

Write on the board: "The difference between a comma and a period is that your girlfriend does not have a comma every month."

DETENTION

There was a prehistoric custom called *detention*. The teacher sat unsmiling at a metal desk at the front of the room. He grunted over papers no one wanted to write or read. The clock over his head looked like the painting of a clock. Its hands never moved for the smart alecks and dumbasses stapled to our seats.

PURGATORY

The floor was the only thing lower than a freshman boy at the first high school dance. The DJ played the Four Seasons, which is how long the night lasted.

———

THAT'S THE TICKET

My mom volunteered to be the ticket lady at Nancy's elementary school. When the kids came up to the table to get a ticket for lunch, she made them give her a kiss.

VALENTINE'S DAY GIFT

Lenie and I pooled our money to buy a gift for our mom. We bought her a white ceramic vanity set decorated with lavender flowers. It included a hand mirror, a hairbrush, a large comb, and a perfume bottle. This infuriated her so much she sent us to our rooms for punishment.

GO FIGURE

My mother was heavy. In high school, I discovered I was attracted to skinny girls. My first crushes looked like pick-up sticks with colorful skirts.

RELIGIOUS CONVICTION

My mother was fervent on the subject. She was unwavering in her faith. She believed girls and women should wear makeup.

Meanwhile, I developed an aversion to makeup. If a girl wore eyeliner, I tried not to notice. If she wore lipstick, I lost interest. Nail polish was a deal breaker.

HANG IT ALL

One of the first things I learned in high school: I was a sucker for an artsy girl who could nonchalantly toss a scarf around her neck.

HYPOTHETICAL

My mom said, "It's just as easy to fall in love with a rich girl as a poor girl." I tested the hypothesis. False.

EYEGLASSES

1.

"I'm not buying you eyeglasses," my mother told Lenie. "Boys don't like girls who wear glasses." I knew for a fact this was not true.

2.

When our mom wasn't around, Lenie borrowed her friend Vicky's glasses so she could see better. Mom accused her of being rebellious.

3.

My mother gave Lenie lessons in how to attract a boy. Lenie walked up and down the hallway with a book balanced on her head. This would elongate her neck and make her look more graceful. "Wouldn't it be better to just read a book?" I asked her. "I can't read right now," she said. "I'm not allowed to wear glasses."

4.

I didn't need glasses. But I liked the balancing game. I walked down the hall with a book on my head too.

5.

I burst into Lenie's room. She was practicing batting her eyelashes in front of the mirror. It looked like a twitch. "What's wrong with your eyes?" I asked her. "I'm talking to Mom. You need glasses."

SCIENTIFIC METHOD

Lenie fantasized about her eighth-grade science teacher, Mr. C. She loved his passion for charts and tables. If only he would explore her, scientifically. Luckily, there were no trials and errors.

————

TAKE A SHOT

I was deadly with a two-handed set shot. I could launch from anywhere.

The varsity coach dropped by freshman practice. "You'll never play for me with that shot," Coach Schnurr told me. "It's old-school. Get a jump shot."

This took him five seconds to decide. It took me a year of practice on the playground. Is that jumping to it?

PEP RALLY

Layf was the shortest player on the freshman B team. Bob was the tallest player on the freshman A team. They were trotted out together at the pep rally. They looked funny standing next to each other. It was like a crude circus act—everyone cheered.

SWITCHING IT UP

I was not a power hitter, but I could spray singles and doubles. "You wait an instant too long on the ball," my freshman baseball coach said, "but you have a knack for going to the opposite field." I lit up. This was even better than therapy! He explained me to myself.

SATURDAY NIGHT LIVE

Lenie and I were babysitting for Nancy. She was down for the night. We were watching TV in our parents' bedroom. I dozed off. I mumbled in my sleep. Lenie couldn't hear the show. She told me to go to bed. I opened my eyes and looked at her. "How can I go to sleep when there is a runner on third base?"

EPIPHANY OF A JOCK AT TWO A.M.

You could never be the most talented, but you could get the most from your talent.

THE BEST TENNIS PLAYER

My friend Gilford was the best tennis player in school. His swing came from nature. He starred on the varsity team during freshman year. Gilford's parents were snobs. His father was a banker, his mother a socialite. Their social lives revolved around the country club. Gilford didn't like the tennis vibe. He quit the team. His parents wanted him to be a banker. He vowed to become a social worker.

HIGH-SCHOOL CHEMISTRY EXPERIMENT

Question: What happens when a friend who understands chemistry won't help a friend who doesn't understand chemistry with his homework?

Answer: An explosion.

Conclusion: Broken friendship.

22

APPRENTICESHIP

My summer job gave me a new appreciation for school. I commuted with my father to work. He acted like he was waking up an entire barracks. Every morning at 6:15, he rapped on my door and shouted, "Drop your socks and pull up your cocks!"

It took an hour to go sixteen miles. The traffic on Edens Expressway was bumper-to-bumper. The car lurched forward and stopped. My dad hit the gas with his right foot, the brake with his left. That's why kids got seasick in the back seat.

My dad listened to talk radio. I didn't know about the crackpots. They made him laugh. They made me wonder.

The 99-cent breakfast at the Y wasn't worth the Christian lecture.

My dad sold boxes all over the city. He could have written a guidebook. He knew every street, every neighborhood. The geography rolled off him. He knew the cheapest place for everything: fresh fruit, gas, tennis shoes, lawn mowers—you name it. He should have had his own show.

He was fit because of his first principle: one does not pay for parking.

Wertheimer Box & Paper Company was located on the west side of the Loop. We drove through Skid Row to get there. This was a twelve-block strip of bars and flophouses. It was my introduction to the down-and-out, the homeless, the hopeless.

My dad was like a sociologist from the University of Chicago. He could spot bums, tramps, and hobos. Bums were winos, tramps tramped around town, hobos hopped freight trains.

There are some people who just want to get lost. Kurt knew a few guys like that back in the day.

He once knew a drunk who carried around a battered copy of *Walden*. Thoreau was one of those guys.

We parked in a gravel lot across the street from the factory. It was filled with broken glass. My dad angled into a spot. He pulled out carefully. It was a magic power. He never got a flat.

My dad would be stunned by the neighborhood now. It is filled with hipster restaurants. The factories have been converted to condos and lofts. We could live where he worked.

All day my dad called on customers. He was on a first-name basis with everyone. Street-level democracy was natural to him. It was something to emulate. He heard America singing.

Whatever it was, whatever you sold, Kurt sized it up at a glance, then drew you a carton. He was like a pitcher who painted the corners. He didn't miss.

My dad didn't let on he was proud of me. But the guys I met all knew I could smack a baseball.

Kurt never cheated anyone of anything. He gave everyone a deal. His boss complained the deals were too good.

My dad's charm was practical. He explained his theory of being a salesman: "You have to kiss some strange asses."

WORKING MOTTO

My dad's maxim has followed me through my working life. It was an accurate forecast. But I have spent much of my life around academics. He had no idea how strange.

TAKING ORDERS

I worked alone. I took orders on the phone. Then I filled them in a gigantic warehouse on the second floor.

I drove a forklift. I ferried skids on a freight elevator to the main floor. Giant machines were stamping out boxes. You didn't want to distract the workers feeding those machines. That could cost someone a hand.

I drove the lift to the loading dock. I talked to Ron. He had fights on Saturday night. He had a metal plate in his head to prove it.

Upstairs, I called trucking companies. When I was done, I climbed high stacks of boxes and read Russian novels about tormented souls. I surveyed the warehouse from above. I scurried down whenever someone came to look for me. I didn't bother when it was my dad.

THE SPRINKLERS

You are trying to jab the prongs of the forklift into a tower of wooden pallets stacked nearly to the ceiling of the warehouse. "Whatever you do, do not hit the sprinklers," you tell yourself, as you lose control of the prongs and hit the sprinklers. Water sprays everywhere. Someone telephones the fire department. Large men in big boots tramp through the warehouse. A ton of boxes are ruined. You're still not fired.

————

BOSS

Ernie Wertheimer was tall and loomed over everyone. He made all the employees nervous, including my dad. To me he looked like a milk carton on stilts.

Ernie's younger brother George went out on his own. He started a rival Wertheimer's. He offered to bring my dad in as a partner. My dad was afraid of the risk. He didn't want the responsibility. My mom called him a coward. There were fights about money, prestige. He wouldn't budge. He wasn't the boss type. Because my dad wouldn't leave Ernie my mom almost left my dad.

My dad considered himself a salesman. He didn't tell people he had been promoted to vice president. My mother did not consider him a salesman. She told everyone he was a vice president.

HOW TO DEPLETE AN ACCOUNT

My dad was afraid to ask Ernie for a raise. He was afraid to tell my mom he didn't ask for a raise. He pretended he got one.

Every two weeks my dad withdrew money from the savings account and added it to the checking account.

Kurt came home at lunch to intercept the mail. One day he was late. Irma opened the statement from the Bank of Lincolnwood. She thought it had made a whopping mistake. She called in a huff. The huff was returned. Kurt got caught.

My mom accused my dad of "piddling" money away. This was a $10,000 piddle. That would be almost $100,000 today.

Kurt got punished, like a kid. Every week his wife doled out the cash. He was stone broke by Wednesday. He emptied his pockets to prove it. I said to my mom, "Give him a break. Dad just checked out."

I got the glare.

KEEPING ACCOUNTS

Irma of Goodies opened a suitcase for her accountant. The receipts flew everywhere, like butterflies with tattoos landing on the carpet. I was passing by. "Promise me that you'll become a tax lawyer," my mom said. "It's the most creative part of the law." She was doing the books, keeping accounts, looking for loopholes.

––––––––

SHOPPING

August meant my mom wanted clothes for her birthday. Lenie and I went to Marshall Field and bought her a pink wool suit with a black velvet collar. She loved it so much she returned it. She went to an outlet store in Kenosha and bought the same outfit. With the money saved, she could afford the blouse too.

The store policy was "No Refunds." But my mom made such a fuss at the counter the manager came over and gave the money back just to get rid of her.

My mother liked to shop at the Lord & Taylor clearance center. Every month they marked down the items that didn't sell. My mom took the outfit she liked from Plus and hid it in Petite. She made sure to color code. She returned to buy it when the price was slashed.

My mom did not think I was a good shopper. She was like a panther surveying its prey. "You've got to have patience," she instructed me, "then you pounce."

"You're going to hate my gift," my grandmother said. "I will not," my mother replied. "I could never hate anything you give me." My grandmother gave her a long package. My mother unwrapped it. It was a new umbrella. My mother put it down carefully. "I hate it."

GOLFING AT STOP N SOCK

My father had a slice. My mother had a hook. I swiveled and swung away from them.

FAMILY BOWLING AT ALL STAR LANES

A blood sport.

THE TOPS

My dad bowled in a league on Tuesday nights. His team was *The Tops*. There were four of them. He had a stutter step and a good hook, like a prize fighter. He could roll 190, 200, 210, not more. He didn't come home with trophies; his guys never won a championship. "My team was misnamed," he said. "We were almost tops."

————

ORIENTATION

During my freshman year, I lettered in football, basketball, and baseball. So, when my mom asked me to show Lenie around the high school before she started her freshman year, I was eager to take her to see my picture displayed on the Wall of Fame outside the gym.

I studied the photographs with admiration. "Any questions?" I asked.

"Just one," she said. "Where's the bathroom?"

Poor Lenie. She was already over it, and she had three more years of my high school games to go. Then there was college.

DOUBLE PRACTICE IN AUGUST

Pads in the morning, no pads in the afternoon. After six hours of practice, I staggered upstairs to bed. I grabbed something to eat on the way. The next day it started all over again at 8 a.m. Coach Henrici walked onto the field and blew his whistle. "Let's hustle up. Nobody walks but the mailman."

PEP TALKS

Coach said, "There is no 'I' in the word *team*." I got thirty pushups for piping up, "There is no 'we' in the word *team* either."

I got thirty laps for saying that when Coach said "No pain, no gain" it sounded like a slogan for Weight Watchers.

Coach said, "Keep your head up and your nose down." I called out, "That's easy for you to say. Some of us have a heavy lift." He let it go.

DEVIATED SEPTUM

Coach Henrici wanted me to breathe through my nose. He ran a mile beside me. First, I started gagging. Then I turned and vomited on his shoes.

My nose did not work well. I could not smell much either. It was all for show. I had a deviated septum.

My family knew I needed an operation. But every time I

brought it up my mother suggested I could get my nose clipped at the same time. I was afraid that she'd have me clipped while I was unconscious.

RHINOPLASTY

My mom never stopped sticking her small nose into my business. Mine was too large for her. I thought it fitted my face. She did not. She tried to convince me to get a nosejob so many times Lenie offered to get one instead just so she would cut it out. My mom refused. Lenie didn't need one.

THE CONTEST

There was fanfare in the family as my cousin Allan and I faced off for the nose contest. The winner was second-best. The loser was the one with the bigger schnoz. Or maybe it was the other way around.

We moved our faces slowly toward each other. We inched closer and closer. You cheated by turning your head. The contest ended when your nose touched the other's cheek.

Allan thinks that I rammed my monster through his cheekbone every time we competed. I recall it differently.

The entertainment was for my grandmother. "I don't know what you boys are carrying on about," she laughed. "You two don't have big noses."

"Not compared to you, Grandma."

The old lady had us beat. Her nose bent in a few different directions. We were amateurs. She could have competed in the pros.

PUTTING THE NIGHT AWAY

My grandmother was having trouble getting her wall bed back into the walnut doors. She was tired and had slept poorly. Bad dreams were still floating around. "I've got to put this night away," she said. We pushed until the darkness was gone.

23

DARK NIGHT OF THE SOUL, HIGH-SCHOOL EDITION

I started crying at unexpected times. I burst into tears on the way to school. I started to write things down to see if I felt better. What I wrote came out in lines. I called it poetry.

EYEWASH

My eyes were red from crying. We had a little blue eyewash cup shaped like an eye. It was vintage. I tilted it back and soothed my sadness with saline.

MY FEELINGS

My feelings were so strong I couldn't control them. They did what they wanted. Sometimes we traveled in different directions. Whenever they got too far away from me, I ran after them.

BOYHOOD NEIGHBORHOOD

Abraham Lincoln said his boyhood neighborhood in Indiana was "as unpoetical as any spot of the earth." He'd never been to Skokie.

In honor of Lincoln, it's best to be honest. My suburb is one place I never planned to write about.

MY NEW VOCATION

Reading poetry, I felt poetry reading me.

I knew what Wordsworth was talking about when he crossed the Alps. That's because Lenie and I used to race up and down an enormous hill in Montrose Park. It was as steep as the Alps. Wordsworth wandered lonely as a cloud. But did he go sledding like us? You skidded fast. You didn't have time to reflect on it.

I didn't like Carl Sandburg because everyone else in Chicago did. His town was long gone. "Hog Butcher for the World"? I don't eat pork. "City of the Big Shoulders"? I'd rather slouch. "The fog comes in on little cat feet"? I'm allergic to cats.

When I was lonely late at night, I climbed out the basement window and circled Laramie Park. I walked past the farthest city light. I recited poems I was trying to memorize. That's how I became acquainted with the night.

I had never looked at the sky, I mean really looked, until I walked around the park at night. No wonder Gerard Manley Hopkins's sonnet "The Starlight Night" has fourteen exclamation points. *Look at the stars! look, look up at the skies!*

I found my grandfather's leather-bound copy of Longfellow's *Collected Poems* on a bookshelf in the basement. The upper-right-hand corner of a page was turned down at "The Jewish Cemetery at Newport." He was sending me a message: "We're still here."

TWENTY LOVE POEMS AND A SONG OF DESPAIR

I worked over Christmas vacation at the box company. I bought my lunch from a truck outside. Then I ate by myself in the lunchroom.

One day Maria saw me reading a translation of *Veinte poemas de amor y una canción desesperada*. She loved Pablo Neruda. I asked her if she could read it aloud in Spanish. We stood by ourselves on the loading dock. It was the most romantic thing I'd ever heard.

Every day Maria held my hand when she recited the love poems. We went outdoors but we didn't have an outside relationship. After twenty days, we hit the song of despair.

PROVERBIAL POETRY

1.

I asked my grandmother if the street where I was born was named after Lord Byron. She said, "I doubt it. I never saw any lords or ladies in that neighborhood."

2.

I left *A Coney Island of the Mind* on the kitchen table. "I took the girls to Coney Island," Grandma said. "They drove me crazy."

3.

My grandmother worried I was becoming like my grandfather. "You have the same tendencies. You think every lens grinder is Spinoza."

4.

She was afraid that I would never earn a living. "You're a dreamer. Just remember that dumplings in a dream are not dumplings but a dream."

HOBBYHORSE

"Stop horsing around," my mom said. "Poetry is fine so long as it sells products. Otherwise, it's just a hobby, and no one gets paid for a hobby."

––––––––

INAUGURATION DAY, 1965

At the inauguration people chanted, "All the way with LBJ." I was fifteen. I thought "all the way" meant something else.

ONE-PARTY RULE

The Skokie Caucus Party has ruled the village since 1965, the year President Johnson signed the Voting Rights Act into law. All power to fair voting in Skokie, where almost no one votes.

NIGHTHAWKS

I took the train downtown to the Art Institute. I walked between the stone lions. I climbed the stairs to see Edward Hopper's *Nighthawks*.

It was 1942. I sat in a diner with a woman in a red dress drinking coffee in the middle of the night. I walked her home afterwards. She had a flask in her purse. We kissed in the shadows. There was no one in the world but us.

A SUNDAY AFTERNOON ON THE ISLAND OF LA GRANDE JATTE

My mom dropped me off downtown. I ran up the stairs so I could linger on a leisurely afternoon by the Seine. No one jostled me. Everyone was polite. I was impressionable, and all those dots made a point: there was another way to live.

STANDING WOMAN

One afternoon, I was rushing out when I saw Alberto Giacometti's *Standing Woman* by the door. She was utterly motionless—tall, thin, remote.

The label said she was made in 1956. She was one of six. To me, she was the only one.

I walked around her. She is not someone to be trifled with. I didn't have time for the Spoon Woman stationed nearby.

Standing Woman is a Swiss archetype. She is ancient, faceless, skeletal, and bronze. I met her many times over the years. I never understood her.

RAPID TRANSIT

I lingered too long. The Skokie Swift was slow on Saturday and broke down at the Howard terminal. Its logo was a swift bird, but I was late walking home. Transit was stymied, punishment rapid.

THE TEST

Lenie and I were deep in high school when Ruby showed up again. We agreed to meet him in a coffee shop at the Purple Hotel in Lincolnwood.

I had never been inside its purple façade. It looked bruised. Lenie had been there often. It was a place where the boys in her class went to become men.

We saw a heavyset stranger sitting in the corner. His hair was silvery white. We couldn't tell if it was him. The man didn't move a muscle. We thought it might be a test. We started out in his direction—that's when he got up and waved.

Lenie ordered blueberry pie. I said, "Uh-oh. You always stain your dress when you eat blueberry pie. You're going to have to get naked."

Ruby reminded us that his son Ellis is exactly ten years younger than I am. His daughter Helen is precisely ten years younger than Arlene.

He said, "Every decade I do it twice and then I'm done." He slammed the table two times: "Bang! Bang!"

PRIME RIB

We saw Ruby one more time the next year when he took us to a restaurant for dinner. He said, "How's your mother?" It was more a snort than a question.

We didn't learn anything about anyone.

The only other memorable thing about the visit was that we could order anything on the menu. We had prime rib. The meat was marbled and tasted expensive.

REACHING OUT

Lenie wrote to Ruby and said she'd like to see him again. He didn't respond. Years later he told her that his handwriting wasn't good. He didn't like to write letters.

ON THE TOPIC OF PRIME RIB

At dinner, my mother scanned the children's menu. She ordered a child's portion of prime rib. She was outraged when the waitress said it was only meant for children.

FIREBIRD

My mom had an image of herself in a turquoise Firebird convertible. She lowered the top and tied a silk scarf over her head. She wore large fashion sunglasses. She could pull off a glamorous look. Hey, everyone, did you see Grace Kelly tooling around Niles and Morton Grove?

ON FLIRTING

Whenever my mom got stopped for speeding, she cried and flirted with the officer. She never got a ticket.

LOVE IN THE AFTERNOON

We lived in a small house. The walls were thin. My parents had to arrange to see each other in private.

My dad drove around calling on clients all day. Sometimes he called on my mom.

I didn't know when my dad made his house calls. But we noticed there were no arguments at dinner. He loved the meal.

Lenie did not believe our parents were doing it in the afternoon. She asked, "How can you be so sure?"

I said, "Mom told me."

LET IT RIP

My parents let it rip at their Saturday-night parties. My dad drank extra dry gin martinis. One time he fell asleep in the bathtub. Occasionally we had to step over him in the hall. Once, when the party was still going, he took off his pants and slept in the living room. It was quiet when we got up in the morning. No yelling. We didn't wake him.

V.O.

My dad's friend Herbie was the national sales manager of Seagram's Extra Dry Gin. After he added Seagram's V.O. to his portfolio, the parties seemed to start on their Very Own.

MY SISTER'S FIRST DATE

We were at the pool at the Fontainebleau. Lenie walked by in a two-piece blue-and-white check suit. My dad bragged about her to a college kid. "That's my daughter," he said. He offered to fix them up.

Leonard was twenty-one. Lenie was fourteen. He was a junior in college. She was a freshman in high school. Lenie said he was too old for her. My mom pooh-poohed the idea. She helped Lenie dress and fix her hair.

Leonard thought Lenie was sixteen. He bribed the maître d' to let them into the hotel nightclub. Lenie ordered a Shirley Temple. He invited her to go deep-sea fishing with him the next day.

In the elevator, my sister was so scared of what might happen she plastered herself against the wall. But Leonard just wanted to borrow five bucks to get his car out of the garage. He used his extra cash for the bribe.

YOM KIPPUR, 1965

God didn't want Sandy Koufax to pitch for the Dodgers in the first game of the World Series.

So long as I fasted, God didn't mind if I watched the game on a black-and-white TV. A color TV would have been too much.

If Don Drysdale had only been Jewish, he wouldn't have gotten walloped by the Twins.

WEST OF EDEN

I was turning sixteen. Things were changing. I thought Jake's Snack Shop was permanent. But then Jake sold the place to Jack, and it became Jack's Restaurant. I sat at the counter. Everything was pretty much the same, but I liked the old place better.

|| 24 ||

PARALLEL PARKING

The guidance counselor was my driver's ed teacher. He liked to talk about football. He didn't guide me much on driving.

I angled the car into the school lot. We never practiced parallel parking. Therefore, I failed the test for my driver's license twice.

I had one more try. I diligently practiced between garbage cans in front of the house. It was like playing bumper tag. I didn't know who got it worse—the fender or the cans.

My dad and I drove to Des Plaines for my last try. I pulled into the street. The instructor had a headache and blew off the part about parking.

I drove to the first McDonald's on River Road to celebrate my special day. It was as spotless as all the others. But there were hundreds of green pickles dotting the lot.

"I guess they don't want you to park here," my dad said.

CAUTION

Whenever I drove, my mother sat in the passenger seat and slammed on imaginary brakes at yellow traffic lights. This was cautionary. When I was on my own, I stopped. When I was with her, I gunned it.

AFTER I GOT MY DRIVER'S LICENSE

I picked up my grandmother at her poker game on Saturday night. She wanted to show me off to her friends. She was in high spirits after the win. When we got back to her place, she drank half a beer to mark the occasion.

My grandmother didn't want me to drink and drive. That was a laugh. I had never even had a full beer. I ate a pastry in celebration.

Whenever I had a date, I dropped off my grandmother in front of her apartment on Lawrence Avenue. She said, "Good luck in all your future endeavors."

"Okay, Gram, but I'll pick you up for breakfast in the morning."

COFFEE-AND

My grandmother took me to Denny's for coffee-and. "You're going to like this," she said. She ordered me a slice of apple pie with a piece of American cheese on top. I pretended to love it. After that, she ordered it for me every time we went out. I pretended to love it for the next twenty-five years.

———

DATE WITH DAWN

Dawn's parents, the Lyons, wanted to know where I was taking their tiny Lyonesse. I explained. They frowned. When would I bring her home? I estimated. They disapproved.

I opened the front door to leave. Dawn was still holding her coat, like a lady. I helped her slip it on. We walked to the car. I sat down in the driver's seat. The lady was still standing outside. The gentleman hurried around to open her door.

Dawn told me to choose a movie. She didn't like the movie I chose. She wanted popcorn. I popped out to get it. She wanted butter on the popcorn. I popped back.

Dawn wanted Milk Duds. I didn't say a word about duds. I had already had Good & Plenty.

I took Dawn to Lockwood Castle on Devon. We sat in a booth by the window. Dawn ordered a large hot fudge sundae. She took two bites and put down her spoon. She was finished.

I had had enough. I told her to eat the whole thing. You'd think she was plowing through the Giant Killer—that had twenty-four scoops with a sparkler and an American flag. Dawn ate one small scoop. This took longer than the movie.

I drove Dawn home. The trip lasted several hours. I walked her to the front door. That was fast.

A FEW DATES

I went on a few dates with Bettyanne. We had bashful back-seat experiences. But I had to give myself a B- because Bettyanne didn't like me as much as Brett Balmer. He was blonder and balmier than me.

I crushed on Karen because she was cute in green culottes.

Hamlet at the movies: To put your arm around her or not? That is the question.

I went to a drive-in movie with Rochelle and her mother.

Not every date likes to go to the batting cages.

Miniature golf is a novelty, not a sport. But Sheryl and I played it like the Masters. She shouldn't have gloated when she beat me with a lucky shot on the eighteenth. I shouldn't have pounded my putter up and down on the green.

We went to Riverview amusement park. I was wobbly on the wooden roller coaster. It was called the Bobs. I turned yellow and bobbed to the bathroom.

It was hellishly hot. The funhouse was called Hades.

A FEW DATES, SISTER VERSION

My mom wanted Lenie to wear more makeup, to put on false eyelashes and fake fingernails, and to bleach her hair blond. Lenie looked at herself in the mirror and said, "Who's that vixen?"

Mom made sure that Lenie had a dime for her dates so she could call home if she got in trouble.

When Lenie's date got too frisky at the drive-in, she climbed out the window. Later, she realized she could have just opened the door.

Lenie had one regret. She was sorry she left her popcorn in the front seat.

Lenie was mad at Phil. She told him to "get lost." He took her literally and couldn't find his way home.

Our front door had a little window. When Lenie stood on the front stoop saying good night to Ron, my mom's face magically appeared. When his friends saw her, they drove away. Ron freaked and fell face down on the sidewalk chasing after them.

Everyone called Randy "the Lamb" because he had curly blond hair. The Lamb told Lenie to stop wearing a short skirt and shiny thigh-high black patent-leather boots. Why? He was upset because he saw her underwear.

Making Fred a flank steak was fine. Cooking it with plastic toothpicks was not.

Neil took Lenie to Lockwood Castle. He ordered tea and toast. He said he had stomach problems. He came back from the bathroom with a wet shirt. He said, "I got whomped by a chocolate soda."

HAIR OF MANY COLORS

My mom was always dying Lenie's hair. It looked like Joseph's coat of many colors. In three years, it went from platinum blond to brunette to zebra stripes. Finally, they stripped all the color. It was white, but looked green because she was wearing a green dress. No one noticed. The next day she dyed it red.

TRACK AND FIELD DAY

Lenie's reputation was shot after she won first place in the shot put. They publicized it in the school paper. Layf kept calling her *Moose* and so Lenie put down the heavy metal ball. An Olympian was lost.

HURRAH!

Horace Traubel called baseball "the hurrah game of the republic!" Whitman thought this was hilarious. From then on, he called it "the hurrah game!" He said that baseball "has the snap, go, fling, of the American atmosphere." Whitman had pep. So did Coach Coyer.

SOPHOMORE BASEBALL

Coach also had a bit of Zen in him. Every afternoon he repeated his favorite koan when we were warming up by throwing the ball back and forth: "Quick but not hard, boys, quick but not hard."

Michael Grejbowski could throw. He was a quarterback who turned me into an end. He was a pitcher who made me regret being a catcher. Grabbo was so fast that I had trouble handling him. I dropped the ball and fired back remarks. He thought they were quick but not hard. We became best friends.

Coyer coached from third base. That left Michael and me on the bench. It was comedy school for high-school baseball players.

Uncle Mel made a mistake. I didn't have the stuff to be a good catcher. I had the wrong physique. I lacked the arm. Runners stole on me. Balls got to the backstop. Coach was on my case. I was getting tired of strapping on the tools of ignorance. It was dumb.

My mother watched me from the fence. "Don't touch your crotch when you crouch."

You weren't superstitious when you got in the batter's box. You just needed to pick up three pebbles and toss them between your legs before you settled down to hit.

MICHAEL AND I

Mine was a two-car family. Michael came from a one-car family. I could get my mother's car on weekend nights. Michael couldn't get his dad's car. Michael and I were inseparable. We had a one-car friendship.

Michael was an only child. He lived down the street from the high school in Morton Grove. Everything in his house was perfectly neat. It wasn't chaotic like my house. I was afraid to touch anything. But it was good to stop there on our way to a double-cheese Whopper at Burger King.

After we dropped off our dates, Michael and I hung out at Booby's on Milwaukee Avenue. We never ordered the Big Boob, but we met Ron, the original Booby.

Michael and I talked about sports and girls. We tried to figure out the score.

We traveled back and forth to Gullivers on Howard Street. The owner, Burt, named it after *Gulliver's Travels*. That's how I learned about Jonathan Swift, "who wanted to vex the world rather than divert it."

The two of us brought our dates for caramelized pan pizza. The four of us talked about sports and books. The two of them told the two of us the score.

Michael and I worked Christmas vacation at Wertheimer. I couldn't read on break. Maria was gone. We played odds and evens on the job: "One, two, three, shoot!" Loser stacks boxes. Loser sweats. Winner watches. Winner gloats.

Michael and I worked during spring break. This time we played rock paper scissors.

My dad got Michael and me a summer job at the Welch Company, which made scientific instruments and apparatus. We couldn't play games. We were supervised.

The bald supervisor told us not to call him Moonhead. He told us not to break any glass instruments. He told us not to screw any of the girls on the floor.

"It's a chemical supply company," he said, "we don't expect you to supply the chemicals."

CHIVALRY AT THE MORRIS AVENUE BEACH

Some burly guy was trying to throw her into the lake. She did not want to go. I didn't know the girl, but I intervened. Michael stood on the side. He didn't budge.

The guy was too big. He spit and hit me in the chest. I spit but missed. He said, "Really?" Then he spit again. I missed him again. I couldn't bring myself to spit on anyone.

It wasn't a genuine fight. We just shoved each other around for a while. The girl went for a swim.

A CERTAIN KIND OF ROMANTIC

Mom said she was a romantic. I gave her flowers for her birthday. "Flowers are a waste of money," she said. "They don't last."

We took her to a Chinese restaurant to celebrate Mother's Day. Mom cried because the food was bad.

25

JUNIOR CLASS PRESIDENT

Everyone was scared by Dr. Nicholas T. Mannos, the first principal of Niles West. Someone upstairs liked him. No one downstairs did.

Our supreme leader was the principal of disproval. He wore a mustard-colored jacket and stood at the back of the gym during basketball games with his arms folded. We never saw him smile.

My classmates decided to give him the finger. They elected me class president.

I was still the rebel who threw things at the president from the back of class. But now I was getting hit by myself.

BELT

I went to the principal's office for student council. I couldn't convince him to change the dress code.

First, I got sent to the principal's office for not wearing a belt.

Then I got sent to the principal's office for scissoring the belt loops off my pants so I couldn't wear a belt.

Then I got sent to the principal's office for saying I wanted to use my belt to strangle the administrator who wrote the dress code that I had to wear a belt.

The principal could not reason with me. But my dad's belt convinced me to change my mind.

IN THE LUNCHROOM

Whenever I wanted to steal something from someone's lunch I said, "Look, there's Dr. Mannos in shorts!" They looked. It worked every time.

I carried this joke over past high school. Even people who didn't know Dr. Mannos still turned around to see him walking by in shorts.

That's how I got a bite of apple, a handful of french fries, a slice of pizza, a fourth of a club sandwich, half a burger, three quarters of a hotdog, and the last piece of birthday cake.

OFFICE VISIT

I dropped by Fairview to see Coach Strongin. He was principal of the school now. I told him my troubles. "The difference is simple," he explained. "A coach wants to see you in his office, a principal does not." We were sitting in his office.

BEFORE AND AFTER A GAME

1.

Gladiators, adjust your pads. Hit your lockers. Crash shoulders. Jump up and down. Storm onto the field. Stay behind the co-captains. Ignore the cheerleaders. Don't wave to the fans.

2.

The locker room is noisy or silent. You cut the tape off your ankles. You stand in the hot shower and watch bruises bloom on your body. You creak into your clothes.

RAH-RAH

I did not like cookie-cutter cheerleaders. I thought they were perky. I liked a girl who worked on Sunday afternoons in the Skokie library. She thought sports books were crude. I liked an art student who said pom-poms were pornographic.

LENIE'S FRIEND

Debbie was related to the Cubs' third baseman Ron Santos. I horned in when she got free tickets to the games. We sat on the third-base side and cheered. He was our favorite relative too.

Debbie's family owned a pizza parlor. Lenie and I liked the pizza, but Lenie didn't like it that Debbie liked me.

I was oblivious. Debbie took me to a Bears game with her family. I thought it was because we both liked football.

––––––––

SEEING MARCIA

My grandmother said I would lose my head if it weren't attached to my neck. It didn't feel attached when I saw Marcia.

Marcia's brown hair cascaded down her back. She walked on the ground like other people, but her beauty was ethereal.

I seldom impressed anyone in my family, but Lenie was incredulous. She said, "That's your girlfriend?"

Marcia was Mr. Paglia's oldest daughter. I cried for her when he died of a heart attack. I didn't know the girl I was crying for. She went to a different junior high school. By the time I met her, Marcia's mother had remarried. Marcia had other reasons to cry.

STAYING HOME WITH MARCIA

Marcia babysat for her six younger brothers and sisters on Friday night. I dropped by as soon as her parents left. Once she got the kids to bed, we necked for hours against the refrigerator. Her front was hot, but her back was cold.

Epididymal hypertension or blue balls. Otherwise known as driving home from Marcia's house on Friday night.

Marcia's parents came home early. They opened the front door. I slipped out the back. What a close call! I started my car and turned around. They were parked behind me.

GOING OUT WITH MARCIA

Marcia's curfew started at 11 p.m. Every month it got earlier. I figured that by the time she was eighteen I would have to get her home by 8 o'clock.

Marcia and I went to the Bahá'í House of Worship in Wilmette. We walked around the nine entrances without ever going in. We sat by one of the nine fountains. We kissed in the spray. We looked up at the dome. I was over the moon.

Driving the winding highway by the lake was close to heaven.

The Grosse Point Lighthouse was our beacon. But it wasn't a good place to park. We stayed away from Harms Woods.

I drove within the speed limit whenever we passed through Kenilworth. It was "Caucasians Only," i.e., no Jews or Blacks.

I went to get fitted for a tuxedo for prom. The tailor measured my waist and then my hips. He did a double take over my slim waist and wide hips. He measured them again to verify. "Hey, Louie," he shouted, "you've got to get out here and see this!"

After the dance, we celebrated with cream puffs in the basement of my house. Our kisses were gooey. I told Marcia that her dress was too complicated. It had taken a stand against me. "My prom dress likes you just fine," she said. "It can stay put."

I got Marcia a heart-pendant necklace from a store in Old Orchard. My mother was so angry I didn't buy it wholesale through her that she grounded me for a week.

I went to church with Marcia's family. No one gave me the instruction manual. I improvised and stood up whenever everyone else knelt.

No wonder Marcia liked "Holy Ghost Square" in Evanston. It has four churches.

It rained at Evanston Beach. I wanted Marcia to laugh. I bought a cheap watch so I could throw it into the waves. The trick worked. When she kissed me on the mouth, time stopped.

MY PSEUDO GIRLFRIEND

Cheryl's parents would not let her date a non-Jewish boy. Every Saturday night I pretended to be her boyfriend. I picked her up and schmoozed with her parents. Then I took her outside to the car. Michael was sitting in the back seat with Marcia. I even gave Cheryl a corsage and took her to homecoming. She has a photograph of us holding hands and beaming for the camera.

––––––––

LAZY SUSAN

Leo Osher, the owner of the Pickle Barrel, boasted that he was the originator of the lazy Susan. He named it after his daughter Suzy. In college, I discovered that Thomas Jefferson made the same claim in the eighteenth century. He also invented a wheeled serving tray for his daughter Susan. It was one of a series of devices—some vertical, some horizontal—that he called a dumbwaiter. But Jefferson didn't give out free pickles and peanuts the way they did at the Pickle Barrel. He was never named Pickle Man of the Year.

SHOW SOME RESPECT

Michael and I once drove his father's pea-green Nova past the Polish Roman Catholic Union on Edens Expressway. He turned down the radio. We often drove my mother's gold GTO past Temple Sholom on Lake Shore Drive. I turned it up.

HOW TO GET A HISTORY TEACHER TO FLIP YOU THE BIRD

He puts on a movie at the beginning of class. This is the third movie day in a row. While he is opening the door to leave, you say, "Thanks for stopping by."

MR. ONE-FORTIETH

I had a good teacher in high school. That makes one for forty. Mr. McMahon taught American literature. He loved *The Scarlet Letter* and looked like Reverend Dimmesdale. He was seriously interested in what he taught. This differentiated him from the other thirty-nine.

LITERARY DISCUSSION

My parents owned a copy of *The Condensed Moby Dick*. They must have gotten it on sale somewhere.

"You can't just read the parts about the whale," I opined to my grandmother. "You have to read the whole thing."

"Uh-huh," she said. "Don't be such a smarty pants."

SHINE ON

I wrote a poem called "Turtle Wax." It had shiny things in it. I had no idea what they meant. I got mad at Lenie because she couldn't figure it out either.

Lenie said, "Why aren't you talking to me? You should have stopped talking to yourself instead."

I punished Lenie by not reading her my poetry anymore. What a masochist! She liked the punishment.

A TOWNIE'S PHILOSOPHY

When you drove east and crossed McCormick Blvd. into Evanston you became instantly more sophisticated.

A townie around Northwestern, I pretended to be a student and hung out at the student center where you could see the lake through a picture window. You never blew your cover if you never talked to anyone.

I snuck into the library for something to do. I spent so much time at the card catalog you'd think I was dating it.

I scoured the open stacks and camped out on the floor. No one stepped over me because the section was deserted.

I wasn't sure if the students were checked out; the books were not.

Thanks to the Dewey Decimal System I discovered Philosophy and Psychology. But I never made it to Psychology.

PROPOSITIONS

1.

Aristotle called God "the Unmoved Mover." It made God sound like the owner of a trucking company. The Boss sits upstairs and pulls strings while employees pack boxes down below. Workers need a Union.

2.

It wasn't Plato's fault. Some Florentine dude in the fifteenth century came up with the idea of *amor platonicus*, the scourge of high-school boys.

3.

"Know thyselves."

4.

"I think, therefore I am." But I wasn't thinking when I made that wisecrack. Does that mean I am not?

5.

What a mess! I had trouble proving I exist, but I couldn't disprove it either.

6.

Ditto for God.

7.

Where can I find a monad?

8.

I may have slipped a biography of Nietzsche into my backpack. I was reading about the theory of eternal return when my parents burst into the room. I returned the book.

9.

At dinner, I wondered aloud if there is such a thing as common-sense reasoning. My dad said, "Yes, you don't have it."

10.

I was puzzling over the idea of universality during the Enlightenment. "You want a universal truth," Mom told me. "Women like shoes."

26

HOW TO WALK

"Take little steps. You walk like a man," my mother told my sister. "Take longer strides," she said to me. "You walk like a girl."

SWISH

"Don't swish when you walk on the court," my mother said. "Swish when you shoot the ball."

The home crowd roared when you trotted onto the court. Everyone you cared about was at the game.

Coach Schnurr said I had the predatory instinct on the press. Coach prided himself on being up to date, but he wanted marauders on the hardwood.

Coach sounded like a general when he talked about playing defense: "Take charge, men, and take the charge."

The general was tactical. He had a wicked underhand free throw. This wasn't the only thing underhanded about his game.

Coach had it backwards at practice. He wanted us to race up the bleachers and coast down them. We wore weighted vests. Mine weighed two thousand pounds. We wore ankle weights. Mine nailed me to the floor.

We were sprinting up and down the court. Coach thought the weights were slowing me down. I wasn't wearing them.

Out of the corner of my eye I can see Michael shaking his hands in the left corner. He looks like he's got the DTs.

Ira had a flattop. He had no arc on his shot and drilled line drives into the hoop.

I was dribbling out the clock at midcourt. The guard from Glenbrook South slapped me across the face. We tussled. The referee broke it up. Coach Schnurr ran out to calm me down. I heard a shrill voice behind me on the court. My mother had come down from the stands. She said, "Are you okay, honey?"

I waved her away. Her voice got louder, more insistent. "I asked if you're okay, honey."

I shouted, "Jesus, Mom, I'm in a fight here!"

BLIZZARD

Six days after my seventeenth birthday, Chicago got hit with its biggest snowstorm. We got dumped with twenty-three inches, and school closed for the week. My mom said, "What's going to happen when you turn eighteen?"

THE MOST IMPORTANT DAY

My mother stood at the top of the stairs. Michael and I were in the dining room. "Your hair looks shaggy," she said. "I want you to get a haircut today."

"No way," I told her. "We're taking the SATs."

My mother didn't budge. "You look lousy. You're getting a haircut right now."

I refused: "This is the most important day of my life."

My mother screamed at me. "You're getting a damned haircut!"

I screamed back. "You're a terrible mother!"

My mother threw a hairbrush at me. I stormed out of the house.

Michael was rattled. He said, "You shouldn't talk to your mother like that. It's disrespectful."

I looked at him. "Want to trade mothers?"

He was mum.

HOW I BECAME AN OUTFIELDER

I was still wearing my catcher's gear in the locker room after the game. A student assistant handed me the tally of passed balls and stolen bases. "I know why we lost," Coach Phipps said, raising his voice. "It's the guy behind the plate."

Coach sent me to right field. It was the right move. The stress indicator went down. The center fielder waved me off most of the fly balls. When I stopped squatting down, my batting average skyrocketed.

SWEET SIXTEEN

My mom threw a fantasy party for Lenie at the Four Seasons restaurant on Michigan Avenue. It was my mom's fantasy.

Mom hired a hypnotist. I was the only boy there. The hypnotist asked me to come on stage while he hypnotized the girls. Lenie watched from the floor. She didn't want to be mesmerized.

First, the hypnotist told the girls that I was the cutest, sexiest boy alive. They flirted and fawned over me. Then he told them that I was the most disgusting boy they had ever met. They grimaced and recoiled. Vicky spit on me.

Lenie and I agreed that my mom's fantasy party was pretty much the worst experience either of us had ever had.

SYMBIOSIS

Lenie's friends liked coming to our house because there were boys. My friends liked coming because of the girls. We thought everyone came over because of us.

DRIVER'S ED

Lenie didn't like her driver's ed teacher, so she got her brother Ed to teach her. They hit the parking lots and highways. She speeded by him and passed her test on the first try.

GARBAGE SUMMER

My parents had connections. My dad got me a summer job as a garbage man in Skokie. It was dirty work. I said I didn't believe in dirty politics. My mom replied, "You're from Chicago. That's the only kind there is."

Lenie and I parted ways. She delivered food and I emptied garbage cans.

I had trouble keeping up with the pros on the route. They did an eight-hour shift in five hours. They needed to finish early so they could get to their second jobs. I raced behind the truck.

When I needed a break, the driver said, "I hope you're good at school, because you're not going to make it as a trash collector."

While I wheezed behind, these guys kept an eye out for the throwaways. They found lamps, tables, chairs, radios. They were like experts at an antique show.

We ate lunch at a truck stop. I didn't know there were truck stops in Skokie. They traded stories. I listened. These guys weren't like my teachers at school. They taught me things.

My own alley was like a foreign country. I didn't recognize my neighbor's houses from the back. Every house was the same. Everyone's crap was different.

I waved to a girl I knew from the back of the truck. She looked at me like at a horror movie.

People didn't see us when we picked up their garbage. They looked past us in the alley. I learned my lesson. It was a daily class in invisibility.

I was trashed. Every day ended at the dump.

I was covered with dirt when I got home from work. "Do you want to know how I feel about this job?" I asked. Then I rolled on the floor.

Lenie said, "Your protest isn't doing any good. The floor is already dirty."

Everyone in the family was relieved when I got mononucleosis. It was better to be tired than miserable.

My skin turned yellow. My mom said, "I told you to stop eating garbage."

I was hospitalized with jaundice. I came home and went to bed for a month. My garbage career was done.

THE HOT CORNER

The sun beat down on Summer League. Coach Phipps gave me a shot at playing third base. It was a magic formula. I gave him three errors.

Do you remember the show *Queen for a Day*? Whoever had the saddest story won. I was "Third Baseman for a Day."

That summer Coach Phipps also tried to convert me into a switch hitter. I gave it a try, but I could never manage to hit both ways.

Coach also taught me to slide headfirst into the bag. That worked because I was reckless.

THE SHORT MANAGERIAL CAREER OF KURT HIRSCH

I was playing Senior League. The manager and assistant manager were sick. My dad took over coaching for the game. He decided to give everyone on the team a chance. In the seventh inning, he sent in the two worst players to play second base and shortstop. They made fielding errors. We lost. In the car home, my dad and I got in a shouting match about fairness. He was for it.

THE LAST RACE

We sprinted on the sidewalk in front of the house. My dad was faster until he wasn't. The last time we raced he elbowed me off the sidewalk at the final moment to take the win.

THE BALLAD OF LENIE AND HOWARD

Lenie met Howard at Morris Avenue Beach. They went on two or three dates before Howard got kicked out of Mather High School for hitting a teacher. He was sent to military school at Roosevelt Academy. Lenie spent homecoming with him and his parents.

Howard had a huge crush on my sister. He wrote her long, gushy, inappropriate love letters every day. Lenie didn't like him much. She thought the letters were boring. He wasn't her boyfriend. She didn't bother to tell him that she didn't want to go out with him.

Howard had a song for their relationship: "Cherish" by the Association. Lenie didn't cherish the association. She renamed it "Cherish Your Fantasy."

One day Lenie came home from school and found our mom sitting at her desk reading the letters from Howard. There was an argument. Lenie wrote Howard a Dear John letter so that our mom would stop snooping around her stuff. Dear John was distraught, Lenie was relieved.

LENIE PENS A POEM

ODE TO HOWIE

Perish is the word that must be applied
To banish all the fantasies, you have inside.
Perish all those sloppy kisses,
All your dreams of wedded blisses.
    Cherish the perish!

UNLOCKED

Our mom didn't get the message. She kept snooping around.

There were no locks on any of our doors. Lenie and Nancy's door didn't even close. Anyone could barge in anytime.

No one did—or almost no one. The kids called "Hey!" whenever we wanted to come in. My father knocked. My mother did not.

"What's going on in here?" she asked. Then she pushed past me into my room.

COUSINS, A TECHNICALITY

Aunt Lil and Uncle Harry had three kids: Bernie, Jeff, and Audrey. One day my mom and Lil cooked up a scheme for Lenie to date Bernie. Technically, they were cousins, but they were not related by blood. The problem was that Lenie and Bernie had no interest in going out together.

MY OTHER COUSIN JEFF

Like my dad, Jeff was short and muscular. He was on the wrestling team. My dad liked to spar with him. They traded holds, locked legs, and rolled on the carpet. Jeff didn't get along with my Uncle Harry. My dad stepped in to help. Jeff was the natural son he might have had.

EARLY INHERITANCE

Michael and I were washing windows for extra cash. I was standing near the top of the ladder. It slipped an inch on the sidewalk. I thought I might fall.

Michael looked up at me. "If anything happens," Michael said, "can I have your record collection?"

It was a modest ask. I didn't have many records.

———

"BREAKING UP IS HARD TO DO"

Marcia wanted to get married to escape her family. I was determined to go to college.

Marcia went to Glenbrook South. I didn't see her all week. I had Lunch every day with Michael and Denise. They helped me chart my breakup. I was resolved. Every Friday night I saw Marcia again. As soon as I saw her, I changed my mind.

I was ahead of the pop singer Neil Sedaka. I already knew breaking up is hard to do.

After six months, I finally broke it to Marcia. We held hands and cried in the parking lot at Old Orchard. No one paid attention until a policeman knocked on the window. "Is everything okay?" he asked. It was not. I tried to speak but couldn't get out the words. He studied us carefully. Marcia was beside herself. "This is not a good spot for a breakup," he said. "Go to the beach."

LAST PHONE CALL

Marcia and I were broken up. I was named to a special All-Conference team in baseball. There was only one person I wanted to tell.

Marcia's stepfather answered the phone. He was not pleased. Marcia's voice was pinched. She was crying. I didn't tell her my news.

Her stepfather got back on the phone. He said, "You are persona non grata around here."

I didn't know the term, but I understood what it meant: I would never speak to Marcia again.

27

HOOKED UP

I moped for months. One night my friends pushed me onto the dance floor at the Hut. They knew a girl who could cheer me up.

Karla and I danced together all night. On the last dance, she put her cross in my mouth. For two minutes, I was hooked up to her necklace.

After that, I tried the Green Gorilla, the Dark Spot, the Pit, and the Deep End, but I never tasted a cross again.

DIANA'S BANGS

Diana was skinny and smart. I was impressed by her perfect 800 score on the SATs. Her outfits were super cute. But it was her arrow straight bangs that felled me. I got banged up on the football field. It was nothing compared to Diana's bangs.

I was fascinated by Diana's face. Her ancestors came from Europe, but she looked vaguely Asiatic, as if they had stopped in Mongolia for a few generations before heading to North America.

Diana was an achiever. She got an A in everything except gym class and boyfriend.

I was less of an achiever—I got an A or B in everything except French class and Diana studies. I was even worse in French than Diana. Failing French was bad. Failing Diana was worse.

I would also give myself a D in observation (I didn't really know what she was like), an F in moderation (I couldn't stay away from her).

After she grew out her bangs, Diana parted her hair perfectly in the center. She kept her looks and feelings under tight control. The unruliest things about her were her appetite (she once ate sixty-four shrimp), her inner life (she wanted to become an artist), and me.

"KILLING FLOOR"

I was a year older than Diana. We dated on and off for six years. I still don't know what made her tick. She said things that other people wouldn't say, but she was also secretive and lived in her imagination.

Diana was a mysterious magnet. I wasn't the only boy who didn't understand why he was magnetized by her.

You could summarize our relationship by saying we got together, broke up, and got back together. Then we broke up again. We couldn't figure out how to be together, but we couldn't release each other, either.

Whenever the commitment seemed too much, I panicked. Then she panicked too. The drama took center stage.

It was bad when other people got involved. Is there such a thing as a semi-breakup? I need a calculator for those. Diana was a math whiz. She could figure it in her head.

Howlin' Wolf's song "Killing Floor" is a Chicago romance. Love is a slaughterhouse.

SAFETY

In football, Michael was good on offense, but he could play defense too. As a safety, he liked to go for the interception. He picked off two of my sister's girlfriends.

TOP-LEVEL NEGOTIATIONS

Many top-level negotiations took place in the car. These involved buttons, bras, belts, body parts, and heavy breathing.

DID YOU FORGET SOMETHING?

After our date, I dropped off Diana and drove home. I poured myself a glass of milk and sat down to read *Sport* magazine. There was a story about a quarterback. This reminded me of something. Whoa, I had forgotten Michael. It was 2:30 in the morning. I rushed over to Lynn's house. It was dark. I rapped on the basement window. No answer. I called out. No response. I rapped harder. I called louder. Still no answer. I decided to leave before I got arrested. Michael had gone home. It was a five-mile walk in the cold. He was not pleased that I had forgotten him. He said something unforgettable.

––––––––––

PSYCHOANALYSIS AND FOOTBALL

My friend Norman was too smart for sports. He said that all the hitting had knocked common sense out of me. He must have been right, because he went to the University of Chicago and became a psychiatrist.

HARVARD TERRACE

I knew a jock who lived on Harvard Terrace. His parents were not academic. No one hit the books. There were better students on Brummel.

DRILLS

One coach called the interior linemen for blocking drills. The other called the backs for running drills. I ran with the backs.

"The ends go with the linemen," Coach Basrak shouted.

"No way," I shouted back. "My mother raised me to study Talmud."

NO SHIT

Dicky and Michael were co-captains of the football team. Michael led the offense, Dicky the defense. Dicky stood up on a bench in the locker room before the Niles North game. He was agitated. He started shouting, "Someone threw a flaming bag of shit on my lawn last night! They defiled my house. Are we going to take that shit? I say NO!"

Michael and I laughed.

Dicky glared at us. He started to chant, "No shit, no shit!" He began thumping his chest and jumping up and down on the bench. It was Cro-Magnon. Dicky shouted at the top of his lungs. Everyone chanted "No shit, no shit!"

Michael and I laughed so hard we started to cry.

ON DEFENSE

I was playing defensive end. During the first half the other team kept running a sweep in my direction. I could not contain it.

First, the tight end blocked me. Then the guard pulled out and hit me. Then the fullback threw himself at my legs. Finally, the ball-carrier cut in front of me for the gain. I did not get help. They scored three touchdowns in a row.

At halftme, Coach Basrak was furious. He picked up a large metal garbage can and pounded it up and down on the locker-room floor. "Hirsch," he shouted, "stop thinking about poetry!"

SPLIT END

I was a tight end, but some formations called for me to split fifteen yards. I trotted out toward the sideline for the snap.

"What's he doing out there all by himself?" my grandmother wondered.

My mom said, "He's loafing in the outfield."

DOUBLE PASS

Squirrel split wide to the left. Michael buzzed him a pass. He caught it and stepped back three yards. I ran for the flag. The defense was caught napping. Squirrel launched one for the ages. I was all alone and raced for the end zone. It was perfect until I got caught from behind on the five-yard line.

TOUCHDOWN

My friend Mike was the announcer for the games. Whenever I scored a touchdown, he shouted over the loudspeaker for my parents to stand up. My dad waved from his seat. My mom jumped to her feet. She clasped her hands over her head like a prizefighter, and everyone cheered.

LITERARY CORRECTION

Years later I wrote a poem saying that I dropped a pass in the end zone because I had a linebacker's helmet imprinted on my back. We lost the game against Maine West. Michael called to straighten me out. "There was no linebacker," he said. "It was a perfect pass. It sailed right through your hands."

TALL BUILDINGS

I caught enough passes to go to a football award ceremony at the Tribune Tower in downtown Chicago. My picture made the paper. There were hulks from all over the city. I was surrounded by tall buildings.

I had to crane my head to look up. This was the American Perpendicular Style.

What I knew about architecture history: First, there was Notre-Dame de Paris. They're Gothic. Then there was the Chicago Tribune Tower. We're neo-Gothic.

You could read about it on the walls. The Finnish architect Eliel

Saarinen lost the competition in 1922, otherwise we would have had a building that looks like a newspaper column. The future was more vertical.

Colonel Robert McCormick, the owner of the paper, really had stones. He had 150 of them embedded in the facade. I was a teenager. I liked the one from the Forbidden City.

Chicago values itself for being level-headed. It dawned on me the city was built up because it was leveled by a fire. We don't do ruins. We build skyscrapers over them.

Form follows function. You can cross the street to the gleaming white Wrigley Building, a castle built for the inventor of Juicy Fruit. The terra-cotta surface even looks gummy.

When I was seven, I saw a movie in which giant grasshoppers climb up the side of it. It's called *Beginning of the End*.

The beginning of the Mag Mile starts at a bend in the river. Or is that the end?

Who doesn't love a movable double-decker bridge? It opened for tall ships and closed for us. My dad and I arrived on the lower level and left on the upper one.

The moon dislikes the dazzle of light. It doesn't feel seen.

Marina City looks modern, but those two high-rises in the round are a tribute to rural Illinois: 120 stories of corn on the cob.

Nostalgia only goes so far. I've never been back to the Drake Hotel, where I became a man. Once was enough.

Michigan Avenue was a boulevard named after Lake Michigan, but it was moved away from the lakeshore after the Great Fire. When did it become all about shopping? The Water Tower was transformed into a tourist office.

Nothing screams political shenanigans like the Blackstone, hotel of mob bosses and presidents: Charlie "Lucky" Luciano or Richard "Tricky Dick" Nixon, take your pick.

On to Ohio Street to celebrate at Uno's. Chicago invented skyscrapers, smoke-filled rooms, and deep-dish pizza.

•

QUICKNESS

Gans was my doppleganger. We looked alike until he got his nose fixed. Then he looked like my mom.

Gans was a track star. He won the 220 at State. He came out for football our senior year. As a wide receiver, he had great speed and terrible hands. He got open for long passes and dropped them. As a tight end, I had great hands and no speed. I caught what I was thrown. The college offers rolled in—for him.

At the dance, Gans thrashed around on the floor doing the alligator. He bum-rushed his friends. He thought it would be funny to take a leak on my leg when I was looking the other way. I felt a warm stream on my pants. I challenged him to a fight. We took it outside. But instead of knocking the piss out of him he beat the shit out of me.

In basketball, Gans led our fast break because he was faster than everyone else. He was also more advanced. At the party, he boasted that he banged Barbara before games. Barbara told him to slow the fuck down.

INTERVIEW TIP TO A HIGH-SCHOOL ATHLETE

Do not tell a school reporter that sports are the second-best outlet for your sex drive. The main outlet won't like it.

FRENCH CLASS

Lenie and I took one class together: French. She sat two seats behind me. My pal Layf had an atrocious French accent. Every time he spoke, I turned around and exchanged a knowing look with her.

Joyce Glick sat between us. She was a good detective. She asked Lenie, "Are you going out with Ed Hirsch?"

Lenie said, "Actually, we live together."

SANTA IN SKOKIE

The class was senior humanities. There were four teachers for eighty students. We broke into small groups. My group chose a topical subject: the commercialization of Christmas. We hit the shopping malls with our cameras.

Everyone filed up to the stage to see our photos of shoppers climbing all over each other. No one liked these photos. Everyone settled back into their seats in the auditorium.

I was team leader. I came up with a title on the way to the podium. I said: "The name of our project is *Does Santa Claus Fuck?*"

I could see Michael and Denise shaking their heads.

The auditorium was still. You could feel the shock rolling through the room. Someone asked a question from the back of the hall: "Are you Jewish?"

The Santa Claus title was the topic sentence in all my classes. My group hadn't noticed we were Jewish. Everyone else did. The humanities teachers were not Jewish. But they belonged to the union. They were radicals too.

My French teacher, Madame Lulejain, was Catholic. She was outraged by my sacrilege. She didn't say anything directly to me. She just tried to ruin my life by failing me in French class. She was appalled by my French. She was more appalled by my religion.

I was called to the principal's office. Dr. Mannos screamed at me. He kept getting interrupted by his phone ringing off the hook. Parents were calling. The students of Young Life were calling. Everyone was enraged that I had desecrated a religious symbol. Dr. Mannos spluttered and called me names. He threatened to have me expelled.

My parents defended me. My mom vowed to take it to the school board. He didn't back down. She said she'd take it to the Illinois Supreme Court. He lowered the charge to a three-day suspension.

Dr. Mannos threatened to suspend the humanities teachers. The union defended them. He didn't back down. They also threatened to take it to court. He dropped the charge.

No one liked my title except art students and future dropouts. They drew cartoons. They slapped me on the back when I walked through the hall.

My parents were boiled. "What the fuck!" my father shouted. "You've got a big vocabulary. Couldn't you come up with another word?"

Christmas survived. Santa was off the hook for another year. He could spend quality time with Mrs. Claus.

My group never forgave me. They were ace students. We each got a C for the class.

THE INFIDEL OF THIRD PERIOD

I liked Cindy and sat next to her in class. One day she told me she was Lutheran. That was fine by me. Then she said that she felt sorry for me because I didn't believe in Christ. "It's so sad," she said, "you're going to hell." After that, we didn't josh around much.

BASKETBALL PHOTO

Coach was pissed off that I had put the team in jeopardy. I had to strap on the weighted vest and sprint the bleachers. I also missed the photo shoot because Dr. Mannos was ripping me a new one. Coach said it was small of me. The photographer made me look like a giant.

THE CENTER

Bob was the center on our team. He was big and patrolled the
paint. We had no idea his father was part of the Outfit until
Mr. G's photograph appeared on the front page of the *Trib*. He
was a Made Man. No one said a word about it at practice. But no
one guarded Bob too closely either.

DUNKED

Evanston was rolling to the state championship. I had never heard
a gym rock like that. I got dunked on for the first time, too. It felt

like someone had pushed my head under water. Bob said it felt like we were wearing cement shoes.

RIVALS

My cousin Earl played basketball for Niles East. We were lining up next to each other for a free throw when he mentioned that Ruby was giving Phoenix a try. I didn't have time to react. The ball went up and he boxed me out.

ANYWHERE

I told Lenie that Ruby was moving to Arizona. She had taken him at his word and forgotten he lived anywhere.

———

HOW TO GET TO PHOENIX

Lenie and I didn't know anything. Our mother knew everything.

In Los Angeles, Ruby worked for Jack Engle & Company. Ruby didn't like working for Jack. He angled to become one of his partners.

Jack found a scrap yard for sale in Phoenix. Ruby surveyed the inventory. It was a goldmine. They went fifty-fifty. Jack provided the stake and stayed in LA. Ruby moved to Phoenix. Jack dealt with Ruby. Ruby dealt with the bank.

Jack and Ruby didn't like managing waste together. Jack went to the bank. He tried to cut Ruby off. The banker didn't know Jack. He knew Ruby. Jack was cut off.

It's hard to double-cross a double-crosser.

After a new emperor was crowned at Empire Metals, the emperor's family moved to Phoenix, where they lived in a tract townhouse. There was something he forgot to tell them. It's hot.

Ruby's office was air-conditioned, but he still sweated over the loamy yard. His style was rough-and-tumble. It takes lung power to close a deal. The rules apply only if you get caught. He kept a sign on his desk that said, ALL I WANT IS AN HONEST ADVANTAGE.

All day the trucks rolled in. The metal baler crushed, cut, and compressed scrap. The sweat furnace melted aluminum from iron. They could have starred in a monster movie.

The director had a good eye for the best junk, and business boomed.

MORE GAMBLING

Ruby couldn't find a good game in his new town. He drove to LA to play poker. The stakes were higher.

Beverly was his good-luck charm, and he took her to Vegas. He liked the Flamingo Hotel because it was the brainchild of Bugsy Siegel. He would have killed to stay in the presidential suite, which had a secret ladder leading down to an underground garage, but he didn't have the muscle.

When he was on a winning streak, Ruby spread the money around. People thought he lost track of what he gave them. He did not.

When he was on a losing streak, he tried not to ask for it back. He succeeded, usually.

Ruby was always up or down at the tables. He was up or down at the scrap yard. He was up or down in the stock market.

Ruby kept the Sabbath in his own way. He read *Barron's* for the financial news every Saturday morning.

Ruby had six or seven bets going at any one time. He was laying money on football games, basketball games, baseball games, and championship fights. He also played the ponies.

There was the occasional side wager, too, like the friend who dared him to quit smoking for a year. For ten thousand bucks, Ruby will-powered that one. But after twelve months, the guy had forgotten all about it. He said, "You should thank me for saving your health," and refused to pay. It took a few years, but Ruby eventually busted him on a deal to collect the debt.

Ruby was like a magician with a disappearing act. When the

pressure got too much, he took off for four or five days. No one knew exactly where he was. But the trick worked. He strolled back into the yard on Monday as if he'd never been away.

My mom couldn't hack it, Beverly managed.

Ruby was a fearless gambler. He could let it ride for the mammoth win. But he had one flaw. He knew it, and so did everyone else. He loved the action too much. He never wanted to leave the craps table, the all-night poker game, the stock market.

Ruby breathed easier whenever he was in the dough. He found it hard to breathe when he was out of it. Money was oxygen.

28

PORTRAIT OF UNCLE SNOOKY

Uncle Snooky was going through changes. He knew people who could hurt you if you called him a schnook.

Snooky had a seat on the Mercantile Exchange. He traded futures for a living. He specialized in corn, cattle, and grains. He was constantly checking the weather, like a farmer.

The markets were volatile. You could never tell if Snooky was up or down—he was usually down—because he acted as if he had money even when he didn't.

My parents complained that Snooky ordered from the top of the menu. It was one of his principles, but everyone else had to split the bill.

When Uncle Snooky started playing racquetball with younger friends, he told us to call him Uncle Maury.

Then Uncle Maury started dressing snazzier and told us to refer to him as Uncle Murray.

Finally, the man who constantly told us he changed our diapers wanted us to stop calling him Uncle at all.

We didn't listen and called him Uncle Snooky.

Aunt Edie always called him by his given name, Maury. He may not have known who he was, but she knew. There was one guy in the world for her. She met him in seventh grade.

PORTRAIT OF UNCLE SY

You would not have guessed Uncle Sy was a war hero. He was part of the Army Air Corps and piloted a C-46 during World

War II. He flew hair-raising supply missions over India, China, and Burma. He had to veer low over the mountains through all sorts of weather. My dad called it "flying the hump."

Uncle Sy was a regular guy who could not hold down a regular job. He opened a bar that failed on the South Side, then flamed out as an exec at Seagram's. He was usually marketing something or other—you could tell by the caps and pens he brought over—but never landed the deal. That's why he moved his family to Savannah to go into business with his brother.

We went to visit on the way to Florida. Aunt Norma and Uncle Sy seemed relaxed in their southern digs. They drank special punch and took us on a riverboat. But there was a problem with the brother. Uncle Sy was changing jobs. He wanted to try mortgage banking.

AUNT IDEL AND UNCLE SHELLY

Aunt Idel lurched forward to tell me a story. I leaned back. I couldn't tell if she was going to block me or tackle me. It was a foulmouthed assault. Like Lenny Bruce, Aunt Idel could really raise the hackles of the censors.

Uncle Shelly chomped on an unlit cigar. To him, Idel was the picture of nobility. He looked at her the way Dante gazed at Beatrice in the earthly paradise.

Everyone loved Uncle Shelly. He wasn't good at business, but he kept finding partners who liked being around him. People wanted to make him rich.

The only person who seemed immune to his low-key charm was his wife. She could take it or leave it. No one was surprised when she left it.

Aunt Idel moved to the South Side. "I stood on the stoop outside her house," Uncle Shelly said. "She wouldn't let me in. I couldn't convince her to come back to me."

Uncle Shelly wanted me to go into business with him, but then he got in hot water for transporting liquor across state lines.

After I went to college, Uncle Shelly followed his son to San

Diego. They hit it big in real estate. He married a mild-mannered woman named Lee and raised money for the City of Hope.

LOVE IS MYSTERIOUS

My Uncle Solly was a cruder version of my natural father—he was Ruby without looks or charm. He got in trouble for certifying non-kosher chickens and moved to Miami to avoid the heat. It was hot there too.

My mom's crowd was loyal to Uncle Solly, but no one much liked him, except my Aunt Phyllis, who adored him from the time they were in junior high. She was devastated when he left her for his secretary Rochelle, who talked like a trucker. Rochelle made Phyllis seem like Queen Elizabeth.

Solly and Rochelle were a match made at the finish line. They loved the racetrack. Their horse was always about to come in.

Rochelle smoked and died young. After that, Uncle Solly got together with a real ding-a-ling and seemed happy.

———

NEW YEAR'S EVE PARTY

"You've got to see this!" Michael shouted. Diana and I rushed to the window. My mother was having trouble getting out of the car. She stumbled backwards into the grass.

My father guided her inside. They paused on the stairs. "Oh, those White Russians," my mother cooed. I had never seen her drunk.

My father was also swaying about. "Let's go to bed, Irma," he said, slapping her on the ass.

BLUE-JEAN SHIRT

My mom tossed my blue-jean shirt into the trash. I fished it out. She took it down the block and tossed it into someone else's trash. I had to try four cans to get it back.

RIPPED JEANS

My mother was standing at the top of the stairs. "Do you want to know how I feel about these jeans?" she asked. Then she started ripping them up.

"Mom," I shouted, "they're not mine! I borrowed them from Michael."

The jeans were shredded. Michael said. "It took me a summer to get them into the right shape, and your mother destroyed them in one minute."

Michael thought my mother was the world's funniest mother. He did not think it was funny when she ripped his jeans. She thought it was hilarious.

THE HARDWARE STORE

We were walking through the hardware store. Michael held up two buckets. "Here's a bra for your mom."

SADDLE SHOES

I borrowed Michael's saddle shoes. I wore them on a date without socks. It took him a moment to notice. He was appalled. "Who do you think you are, Gauguin?"

AT THE BANQUET

Michael and I are the same height. We stood next to each other in front of the head table. Coach handed each of us our photos. We opened ours. Michael was crouched over in a dribble. He looked like he was five feet tall. I was standing straight up. I looked like I was seven feet tall.

We traded photos. Michael was tiny, I was gigantic. This was so incongruous that we started to laugh. Coach glared at us. This was funny and we laughed harder. Coach told us to cut it out. This was even funnier.

Our laughter was so loud that Coach had to stop the proceedings. We were out of control.

We tried not to look at each other but we could feel each other shaking. To keep from going into convulsions, we turned around and put our heads down on the head table. When we looked up, Dr. Mannos was scowling. This made us laugh even harder.

We swiveled around and saw my mother. She was livid. We were in hysterics.

Everyone else was glaring at us. Coach was unable to talk.

We laughed so hard that we had to run out of the room.

PHOTOS REEXAMINED

The next day we showed the two photos to kids at school. "You're going to die laughing when you see this," we said. Everyone shrugged. No one thought it was funny.

GUIDANCE COUNSELORS

I walked two miles in the dark to play pickup basketball with the guidance counselors before school. They knew how to bounce pass to a cutter on offense and box out your man on defense, but they gave me no guidance about college.

TWO FOOTBALL COACHES

Mike Basrak came from a mining town in western Pennsylvania. Football was his way out of the mines. He believed in college football the way his people believed in the church of Christ.

Coach Basrak called me a "freaky kid." He wanted me to play college ball. He said, "I've got to get you off this collision course with coaches." He looked for a freaky school where a freaky kid could play football.

I flew out to Dartmouth College. I didn't know it was an all-men's school until I arrived. They had fraternities. I did not want to join one. This was not what the freaky kid had in mind.

Coach found the Midwest Conference. He convinced my parents to let me apply to Coe, Cornell, and Grinnell.

My father and I drove to Iowa. The prairie grass was high, the fields quilted green. It was how I imagined Ireland, but with more corn and bigger truck stops.

We stopped for a sandwich in Davenport, Iowa, where Otto Frederick Rohwedder invented sliced bread.

I did not like the coaches at Coe and Cornell. They were straightlaced and liked to run the ball.

At Grinnell, we met Edd Bowers. His mother put a double *d* in his first name to honor his uncles, Edward and Edwin. That was my kind of quirk.

Coach Bowers had graduated from Grinnell. He knew what he was getting into. It was the late sixties. He had a whole squad of weirdos.

Coach said that at Grinnell football was so far out it was in. Everyone came to the games.

Coach wanted me to catch passes and hit books. He had seen my film. He was forward looking and believed in the forward pass. He told me I could be his wingback. He had studied the numbers, too, and talked to the financial-aid office. That convinced my parents. We wouldn't have to pay.

WORLD-CHAMPION TALKER

My dad and I went to see the athletic director, Mr. Pfitsch. He was going to be my freshman football coach, too.

Coach Pfitsch was a world-champion talker. I'd put him up against anyone. I'd even bet on him against my mom's friend Yudi, who had recently crushed the competition in Indiana. He had stuff to talk about too, like growing up in Kansas, or fighting in World War II, or taking a sabbatical in India. It was hard to get a word in edgewise.

Coach believed in Zen football. He preached perfect concentration. "I'll tell you all about it when you get here," he said, and he did. He was a college education all by himself.

CAMPUS TOUR

My dad and I walked around campus. It looked the way college is supposed to look. I forgot to ask about academics.

LESSON IN DIALECT

I didn't know I had an accent until I heard people say Chi-*cah*-go instead of Chi-*caw*-go.

GO WEST

Americans know that Horace Greeley said, "Go West, young man!" Not many realize that he said it to Josiah Bushnell Grinnell.

Pastor Grinnell was a railroad builder. He cofounded a town located at the junction of the Rock Island Railroad and the Minneapolis and St. Louis Railway. He figured it would be the railroad hub of the country. That turned out to be Chicago. He was off by 286 miles.

My mom implemented the 300-mile rule. You must go to college within driving distance. She didn't want to pay for flights home. Grinnell qualified. It took four and a half hours to get there.

My mom thought it was funny when we cruised into such a small town. Population: 8,400. Grinnell billed itself "the Jewel of the Prairie." She said, "I know genuine jewelry, and this isn't it."

Gertrude Stein famously said about Oakland, "There's no there there." My mom had never heard of Stein, but the first time she saw Grinnell, she paraphrased her anyway. She said, "There's no here here."

DIVISIONS

Michael was going to Drake University on a football scholarship. He was Division 1. I was Division 3. Des Moines is about an hour's drive from Grinnell. Too bad neither of us had a car. Michael had a strong arm, but it was a fifty-six-mile throw.

CE N'EST PAS BON

Madame Lulejain was still on a tear about Santa Claus's mating habits. She gave me an F. She preferred the French system. Then she could have given me 0 out of 100.

Mrs. L. went down to the principal's office to study my transcript. She was disappointed she could not keep me from graduating. I had enough credits. She gets credit for persistence.

It made Madame mad I was accepted to a good college. She called Grinnell to see if she could get my scholarship revoked. She spoke to the registrar, the assistant athletic director, and the associate dean of students. She talked to more people at Grinnell than I did.

Odette de Lecluse was my French teacher in college. Grinnell is a small place. She had heard about Madame Lulejain. "I don't know what you did to her," she said. "Ce n'est pas bon."

29

PERFECT SCORE

My dad got me into sports. He never said much, but he came to every one of my football, basketball, and baseball games for four years. Sometimes he was the only Niles West fan on our side of the field. I took it for granted, but he must have moved a lot of stuff around to get there. Then he kept it up in college.

I WANT TO BE LOVED FOR MYSELF

"You're so naïve," my mom told Lenie and me. "No one will ever love you for yourself." My mother should have been an actor. She believed that people loved you for being someone else. Our house was like a set. I wonder how much she was staging her own life.

ADVICE COLUMN

While my parents were thinking about my future, I was writing an advice column for the school paper:

"It's not hard to get good grades but finding a good place to make out can be difficult. During the school day, an empty classroom will do in a pinch. A bathroom stall is risky but possible. Janitors have closets."

THE VERDICT

Michael's girlfriend Judy went on vacation with her parents. She gave Michael the key to her house. Diana and I headed to her parents' bedroom.

A Lincolnwood policeman was watching the house. He stopped when he saw a light. Michael was watching TV. He answered the door.

I jumped up and got dressed. Diana panicked and stumbled into a closet. The policeman stomped upstairs. I could not stop him at the door. He flashed a light into the dark closet.

Diana came out naked. The cop clucked. He said, "Well, what do we have here?" He watched her get dressed.

The policeman knew Diana's parents. Her father was a judge in town. The gavel came down hard. Judgment was swift.

THE STUPIDEST THING

The stupidest thing I've ever done was to sniff glue out of a paper bag with three idiots in the back of my friend Mark's car while we were driving around Lincolnwood on a Saturday night in the spring of my senior year of high school.

BEACH BREAK

My friend Joey liked to surf at night. It was illegal, but the daredevil put on a wet suit and waded into Chicago Breaks. Sometimes I'd sit on the jetty and watch. When the wind swelled the waves, he looked like a seal standing up in moonlight.

ALL-NIGHTER

Jimmy and I lied to our parents so that we could stay out all night. We had nothing to do. We walked around aimlessly.

It was 3 a.m. I needed to take a whiz. I walked up to someone's hedges. My pants were too tight. I pulled them down. A police car buzzed around the corner. The bullhorn came out. We were arrested.

The policeman called my parents. My mother answered. I heard my father in the background, "Leave him there."

My father did not leave me there. He rushed into the police station and started slapping me around. The policeman pulled him off me. He threatened to arrest him too.

We drove back. My father kept reaching over and whacking me. We pulled up to the house. I saw my mother at the front door. She was wearing a sign on her face that said, "No Mercy."

I opened the car door and took off. I ran across the park. Then I started hitchhiking on Touhy Avenue. I had no idea where I was going. I was an outlaw heading west.

My westward adventure reached Elk Grove Village. I called home. It was 7 a.m. Sunday morning. I disguised my voice and asked for Lenie. My mother said, "Drop the fake accent. You're not a good actor. Just come home."

My mother had taught me one thing: how to negotiate a settlement. No grounding, no punishment.

My parents picked me up. We went to the police station to prove that I was not a missing person. I wasn't sure of that. I slept for eighteen hours.

DIANA AND DENISE

My desperation to get out of the suburbs blurred my eyesight. I didn't know what people were like.

Diana was so thin I couldn't see her very well. That's when I started to see Denise. She was thin, too. When she turned to the side, I didn't see her either.

Diana was deceptive. She seemed like an angel. Denise was less deceptive. She seemed like a fallen angel.

DENISE AND I

Dns & I tk spd rdng. It spd r ksng.

I could never settle on Denise as a girlfriend. She was Trouble because she was troubled.

Denise said her father's roar turned her mother into a mouse. She explained, "It's worse than you think." She was talking about her family. I had a high schooler's insights. It would take a psycho-analyst to unravel the damage.

Denise introduced me to pop art. She drew Donald Duck deranged. She made Mickey Mouse look like a murderer.

Denise's favorite donut: devil's food. Her favorite poem: "I like a look of Agony."

Denise had all her wisdom teeth removed at once. I visited her at home. It was my first time in her bedroom. I sat next to her on the bed. She looked like a chipmunk in a sexy nightgown. I said, "You look cute." She mumbled, "Sometimes you act like a high-school boy."

I told Denise I still had my old Wham-O Slip 'N Slide. She said, "Is that what we're calling it now?"

"If your backside is termed a *caboose*," Denise reasoned, "then your front should be called a *locomotive*."

Diana and Denise were in my sister's class. My mom knew them both. She liked Diana. She didn't like Denise. She thought Denise was too caustic. That was rich. The pot was calling the kettle sarcastic. The kettle whistled back.

TWO BREAKUPS, ONE DAY

My mother got nervous when she bumped into Diana and Denise waiting for a bus together outside the school. "If you girls are going to date my son," she said, "you should know he is not always truthful."

SATURDAY NIGHTS WITH STEVIE

Diana and I were dating other people. On Saturday night, I stopped by her house to pick up her younger brother Stevie. We went to Dairy Queen on Devon. He ordered a banana split. We drove around for a while. He said, "I could wolf down another chocolate cone." We went back to DQ on D. We drove around some more. Stevie and I were hanging out on the stoop when Diana came home with her date. They had to step over us to get into the house.

Diana was not overjoyed when I took her little brother for donuts at Amy Joy. Another Saturday-night date, another awkward meeting on the stoop.

Diana has a younger sister named Sarah. I hung out on the stoop with her, too. Sometimes their mother, Margaret, also came out for a chat.

Stevie and I stopped going out on Saturday nights when I started dating his sister again. He always called me Brother Ed and said I made the wrong choice.

WAVE IN THE RELIEVER

Michael and I were late for practice. I drove him from the locker room to the pitcher's mound in my mother's convertible. "Now that's how you bring in a pitcher!" Coach Phipps was livid. He ordered us to start running laps around the field. We ran for forty-five minutes. The car stayed parked in the dirt.

LAYING DOWN A BUNT

Coach taught me how to Squeeze and Sacrifice. He knew what he was talking about. At fifty years old, he batted first and played center field for our semipro team.

LOOK ALIVE!

From right field, I could see my mother sitting in her convertible in the parking lot. She hit the horn whenever she thought I was daydreaming. This happened so often that Coach told her to cut it out. "Okay," she said. "But you've got a whistle, Coach. Use it."

MY ABORTED MINOR LEAGUE CAREER

A scout from Pittsburgh came to see Michael pitch. My dad sat next to him in the stands. I got three singles. My dad badgered him so much that the scout offered me a tryout with the Gulf Coast League Pirates just to get rid of him. I didn't go for it. I didn't have the stuff to be a professional Pirate.

TRIP TO LAKE GENEVA

We made our move as soon as the family left for the weekend. Diana and I went to my parents' bedroom. Michael and Judy hit my sisters' room.

After twenty minutes, my dad realized that he was wearing two different shoes. They turned around and came home. Lenie rang the bell to warn us.

My mother tried to push past me in the hallway. I blocked her. She screamed and beat me in the chest. It didn't matter. I was not going to let her into her room.

My mother whirled around. "I see you, too, Michael, don't even try to get away!"

My mother finally retreated down the stairs. Diana and I made the bed.

My parents threatened to call everyone's parents. They didn't call anyone. We left the house. They went to Lake Geneva.

My dad forgot to change his shoes.

––––––––

"STUDYING"

My grandmother gave me the key to her apartment so I could have a place to study. Diana and I watched her walk to the "L" to go downtown. We pulled the wall bed out of the wall.

I lost my virginity the old-fashioned way: in grandmother's bed.

My grandmother was fastidious. I decided to warn her that I had taken down the Murphy bed. I couldn't remake it to her standard. There was also the matter of the sheets. I told her I was taking a nap. She said, "It was a busy one."

WHY THERE IS NO CANDY IN THE CANDY DISH

My grandmother's burnt-orange candy dish was filled with chocolate drops. It is the only possession of hers that I still own. I keep it empty because I am terrified of dropping it.

AT THE BUZZER

Michael rang the bell to my grandmother's apartment. I hit the buzzer. He rang the bell again. I hit the buzzer again. This happened five times until I ran downstairs to get him. We lived in the suburbs. He had never been in an apartment building with a buzzer before. He didn't know how it worked.

PROM DRESS

My mom decided to take Lenie to Levine's for a prom dress. While Lenie tried on dresses, Irma and Elaine chatted away like old friends. It was a one-off. We didn't hear about Aunt Elaine again until Ruby came back into our lives. But Lenie got a turquoise-blue sleeveless dress with a chiffon overlay. Elaine gave them a discount.

WOMAN ON TOP

"The missionary position is for missionaries," Diana said, and flipped me on my back, like a record that sounds better on the B side.

DANCING ON THE GYM FLOOR

The band played "Hold Me Tight." Diana and I held each other as tightly as possible. Then they played "Born to Be Wild," and we flew apart.

THE EXPLANATION

At graduation I told Michael that I had two fathers. He was shocked. He didn't know about my birth father. He spotted my mother in the audience. "That explains it," he said. He didn't say what it explained.

GRADUATION PRESENT

Lenie gave me a Panasonic tape recorder for graduation. The first thing I recorded was her telling me it cost seventy-five bucks.

COMEDY

We were posing for a photo. "Don't get swept away," my mother said. "You look like a broom handle in a black robe."

My parents were discussing their favorite comics. My dad liked Red Skelton. My mom liked Mel Brooks. Red didn't stand a chance.

I asked my mom if she had ever gone to the Catskills to hear the Borscht Belt comics. "Why would I do that?" she said. "I have a family here."

I wanted to expand my horizons. "Someday I'd like to try stand-up," I told my mom. She said, "Now that's funny."

‖ 30 ‖

A LIFETIME

It was my last summer before going to college. I couldn't wait to leave. It seemed as if I had been confined to Skokie for my entire life.

I assumed I could return whenever I wanted—my family would always be there.

My parents had other plans. After Nancy went to college, they moved to a condominium in Northbrook.

Skokie was still there. We weren't.

FAMILY OUTING

My dad loved Mayor Richard J. Daley, who had been reelected again. I despised Mayor Daley. He said that Mayor Daley kept the city clean. I said that Mussolini got the trains running on time.

The Oedipus complex expressed itself at family outings.

My dad and I had our biggest blowup after a golf game. He played badly. I played worse.

My father was driving. He said, "Mayor Daley keeps this city safe."

I made the fascist salute: "Do we have to say *Heil Daley*?"

Kurt turned around and shouted at me. My mom told him to keep his eyes on the road.

He pulled into the parking lot at Niles West. My sisters cowered in the back. I thought he would slug me. Instead, he stormed off in one direction. I stormed off in the other.

My mother jumped into the driver's seat and drove home.

SUMMER LEAGUE

I read Mike Royko's book *Boss* in my baseball uniform in the back seat of the car. It was an exposé of Mayor Daley's corrupt political machine. My father eyed me in the rearview mirror. Finally, he wheeled around in disgust. "Your uniform is filthy!"

HOW IT WAS

Richard J. Daley was first elected mayor when I was five years old. I couldn't recall a time when he wasn't the Boss. I couldn't imagine a time when he wouldn't still be the Boss. It seemed like he was mayor for life.

I was about to go to college, and yet I still couldn't imagine a time when my parents didn't boss me around. I wondered if I would ever stop arguing with them about who was boss of me.

OVERTIME

The Democratic Convention was in Chicago. This was a defining moment of the late sixties. I had to work overtime and missed it.

I mingled with stragglers afterwards. I smoked a joint with a couple who were joining a commune in western Canada. They invited me to join them. That was too communal for me.

I got in an argument with a teenager from Cicero. He was a new marine. He was getting shipped somewhere. He was hazy on the details. He couldn't wait to fight in Vietnam or Cambodia or someplace like that.

Freud said there are no accidents, but I almost corkscrewed the car when a motorcycle skittered on the gravel under the overpass and veered toward me.

I had to babysit for Nancy and took her to Grant Park the day after the riots. There was debris everywhere. We could smell tear gas. It was hard to figure out what had happened.

What had happened was History. It took place while I was on the job.

CHECKUP

My last visit to the pediatrician. The two Robins, Leon and Sid, had been my doctor for eighteen years. After my mother gave birth, they took delivery.

My family started seeing them in Hollywood Park. Then they moved to Skokie, too, as part of the migration.

The Robin brothers took care of Lenie when she was sick. My mom had considered suing them for malpractice, but she still wasn't ready to let go.

I sat on a small chair in the waiting room with five- and six-year-olds. Toy trucks whizzed around the floor. There were scoldings and tears. The receptionist offered me a Dum-Dum.

"LITTLE BOXES"

I turned on *The Midnight Special* for folk songs and farce. The song "Little Boxes" kept popping up on the airwaves. Everyone knew Pete Seeger's version, but this one had just been released on the album *Malvina Reynolds Sings the Truth*.

Reynolds wrote the song on a drive through Daly City in Northern California. The satire describes suburbs where everything looks alike. Everyone acts alike too.

I grew up like that. All the tract houses in our development were little boxes made of ticky tacky filled with oddballs trying to conform. People pretended to fit in.

I liked the simple lyrics, which are catchy, but I also hated them for being superficial. Malvina Reynolds did not sing the truth.

Driving through a place is not the same thing as living in it. People were not leading cookie-cutter lives. It only looked that way from the outside.

Your little boxes were so much stranger than the sermon, Oh, Skokie. You had engraved yourself on my heart.

"HOME SWEET HOME"

It was as if a farm boy planted his feet in soft blue clay and hoisted a city kid on his shoulders. A tower soared on a strong midwestern back. This was Adler and Sullivan's Auditorium Building for the New World.

Adelina Patti brought down the house in December 1889 when she sang "Home Sweet Home." Jimi Hendrix tried to burn it down when he shredded "Fire," "Purple Haze," and "Wild Thing" in August 1968.

I drove home along Lake Shore Drive. The buildings bright on one side, the lake dark on the other. I played apocalyptic songs on the cassette. It was a breezy night in the Windy City. I wished it would never end.

"THE LAST GUEST"

My mom threw a party before I left for college. All my aunts and uncles came over to celebrate my going away.

Aunt Edie reminded me that she almost fainted at my bris. Uncle Irv dozed on the couch—it was a hard week at the store. Uncle Jackie slipped me a Benjamin.

My mom's old friends were all about forty years old. Everyone was still carrying on. To me, they'll always be enshrined in middle age.

I felt that something momentous was about to happen.

I wrote a poem about the party called "The Last Guest." Lenie and I both remember how the poem started: "Later, when the last guest flickers and dies." We can't recall how it ended.

The next day I read the poem to my mom. She said, "We must have been at different parties."

POLITICAL SCIENCE

My mom sat me down for a final talk. "What are you going to study in college?" she asked.

"Oh, heaven help me."

"It will, honey," she said. "God needs a good attorney."

SOME ADVICE ON GOING TO COLLEGE

We were playing cards. My grandmother looked agitated. She said: "I'm worried about you. You don't have good judgment."

"Come on, Gram," I said, "you taught me well. My judgment is fine."

This did not reassure her. She said, "I want you to promise me you won't ride a motorcycle. It's dangerous."

I promised.

She said, "Don't become an atheist. It's a bad bet."

She didn't ask, and I didn't promise.

LEAVING HOME

My parents were putting the last bags into the car. My sisters had already scrambled into the back seat. But I was still in the house. I stood at my bedroom door and burst into tears. It was so small. All my thoughts were crammed into that room, all my feelings. I would have to come back to collect them later.

CHILDHOOD WAS GONE

I wanted to get out of there, but I also wanted to hold on to there. It was too late. There was no longer a there. It was lost in time. Childhood had been over for years. I hadn't noticed.

EPILOGUE

Czesław Miłosz claims that once a writer is born into a family, the family is finished.

ACKNOWLEDGMENTS

THREEFOLD APOLOGY

This book tries to capture a world that's gone. My three parents are dead now. I could not have written this when they were alive. They were characters who could tell a story. I've tried to stand up to get something of them down. Gertrude Stein said, "Remarks are not literature." I hope my family proves otherwise. I've done what I could with what I was given.

MY TRUE AUNT

My Auntie Bea (Bernice Allweiss) was a blessing from my childhood. We always knew that we could go to her because she was a saner version of my mother.

At my mother's funeral I said to her, "You talked to my mom every day of your life."

Bea said, "Yes, except the times she wasn't talking to me."

In old age, my aunt forgot that her older sister had died. It was too much to bear.

HOW TO REMEMBER CHILDHOOD

This book is dedicated to my sister Lenie. We lived through everything together. We share a sense of humor and a history. She has vetted my stories, but she also remembers our childhood as traumatic. I prefer to recall it otherwise. Her way was more expensive. It required psychoanalysis.

ADJACENT CHILDHOOD

This book is also dedicated to my sister Nancy, who shares so much of this story. We were raised as one family, but she is young enough to have had a healthier childhood. As a result, she believes in family life. She doesn't just work all the time like us.

BONUS MOTHER

Special thanks to Beverly Rubenstein, my bonus mother, who answered my questions with her remarkable joie de vivre. She has great tales about her life with my natural father. I listened with relish and have used them to flesh out the story of my family. She encouraged me to retell them from my own point of view. She also embraced my unexpected zingers. We have had so many joyous laughs together.

REALITY CHECK

Michael Grejbowski and I did almost everything together in high school. We bonded during sophomore year and have been life-long friends. He has given me a bracing reality check as I've gone through our stories together. He was especially entertained when I returned to Skokie to measure the distance between my old house and the house next door. "You embellish every story," he said. "Why would you suddenly need to nail down a random fact like that?" I've been enriched by his keen memories.

FIRST ENTRIES

André Bernard came into my office. I said, "Listen to this." Then I read a few short pieces. He laughed. He said, "These are very funny. This should be your next book."

THE WRITERS' ROOM

I called Garrett Hongo to read him a few entries. We have traded manuscripts for forty years.

Garrett said, "It was funnier when I heard it the first time."

I called back. Garrett said, "That's too wordy. Focus."

I kept calling back. You can tell a good friend. He answers.

Garrett said, "It's good but tighten it. Read it to me again."

Garrett said, "I don't get it. That's not funny."

He said, "No, do it this way. It needs more punch."

He said, "That's funny. I want the credit for that."

He explained, "Yiddishkeit *is* American humor."

He said, "It's just like being back in the writers' room in California. The Jewish writers used to cut me out. You dig? You're giving me another chance."

Garrett busted a laugh. He said, "You got me with that one."

TWO FRIENDS

As the first person to read the entire manuscript, Nic Christopher gave me an enormous boost. When he speaks about his childhood, I feel as if I've got a slew of Greek relatives.

Rob Casper and I traded stories while we walked around Prospect Park every Saturday. He grew up in a Catholic family in a small town in Wisconsin. It was different.

APOLOGY TO EVERYONE ELSE

I've changed a few names to protect the privacy of people in this book. I'm sorry if I've hurt anyone's feelings. This is not by design. Nor do I mean to desecrate the memory of anyone who is no longer alive. I love the humanity of everyone here. I know my stories get away from me. I go too far. If it makes you feel better, I made myself uncomfortable, too. But that was intentional.

AUTOFICTION

It's like driving a memoir over a cliff. Whenever I veered too close to the edge, I pulled myself back and got in the correct lane. But I can't resist a good comeback. Soon I started quipping past myself again.

SOURCES

I have consulted many books and websites about the history of Chicago, Jews, Chicago Jews, Jewish gangsters, American suburbs, the North Shore, and Skokie. I have gotten especially useful tips from the archives of the *Chicago Tribune* and the *Encyclopedia of Chicago*. Two books have been invaluable: *Skokie (Images of America)* by Amanda J. Hanson and Richard J. Witry, and *Skokie: A Centennial History* by Richard Wittingham. These books give the village a boost. Mine gives it a spin.

AGENCY

Special thanks to my dear friend and agent Liz Darhansoff. I did not expect her to find so much of my early life recognizable. Now that's a story. I hope she tells it. I'd like to represent her.

EDITORIAL

I owe a debt of gratitude to my friend and editor Deborah Garrison, who understood immediately that I was writing a stand-up comedy that is also an elegy for a time and place. She said, "It's poetry adjacent." Our work together is a sustainment of life.

COMEDIES END WELL

Laurie Watel knows my stories. We did not talk much about this book while I was writing it. But we did get married.

Edward Hirsch, a Chicago native and MacArthur Fellow, has published ten books of poetry, including *The Living Fire*: *New and Selected Poems* and *Gabriel*: *A Poem*, a book-length elegy for his son. He has also published eight books of prose, among them *How to Read a Poem and Fall in Love with Poetry*, a national best seller, and *100 Poems to Break Your Heart*. He has received numerous prizes, including the National Book Critics Circle Award and the National Jewish Book Award. He taught at Wayne State University and the University of Houston. Since 2003, he has been president of the John Simon Guggenheim Memorial Foundation. He lives in Brooklyn.

A NOTE ON THE TYPE

The text in this book was set in Miller, a transitional-style type-face designed by Matthew Carter (b. 1937) with assistance from Tobias Frere-Jones and Cyrus Highsmith of the Font Bureau. Modeled on the roman family of fonts popularized by Scottish type foundries in the nineteenth century, Miller is named for William Miller, founder of the Miller & Richard foundry of Edinburgh. The Miller family of fonts has a large number of variants for use as text and display, as well as Greek characters based on the renowned handwriting of British classicist Richard Porson.

Composed by North Market Street Graphics,
Lancaster, Pennsylvania

Book design by Pei Loi Koay